Top 25 locator map
(continues on inside
back cover)
←

D0673764

TwinPack
Malta & Gozo

PA____ & SEA_____ Pat Levy and Sean Sheehan

have written a number of travel
guidebooks, includ___ *Malta,
Seer___ of Turkey, Xi'an, Beijing Street,
CityPack Hong Kong* and
CityPack Beijing. They are now
based in London but now
home in west Cork, Ireland.

7 8

AA Publishing
Find out more about AA Publishing and

If you have any comments
or suggestic__
you can con___
Twinpacks@

0749 543426 5007 2B

Contents

life *5–12*

how to organise your time *13–22*

top 25 sights *23–48*

About this book 4

best 19–30

where to… 61–83

travel facts 85–92

3

About this book

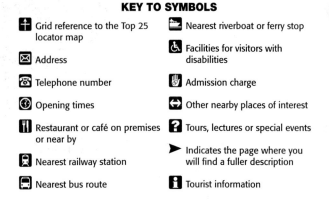

KEY TO SYMBOLS

🔢 Grid reference to the Top 25 locator map

✉ Address

☎ Telephone number

🕐 Opening times

🍴 Restaurant or café on premises or near by

🚆 Nearest railway station

🚌 Nearest bus route

🛥 Nearest riverboat or ferry stop

♿ Facilities for visitors with disabilities

✋ Admission charge

↔ Other nearby places of interest

❓ Tours, lectures or special events

▶ Indicates the page where you will find a fuller description

ℹ Tourist information

TwinPack Malta & Gozo is divided into six sections to cover the six most important aspects of your visit to Malta & Gozo. It includes:

- The author's view of the islands and their people
- Suggested walks and excursions
- The top 25 sights to visit
- Features about different aspects of the islands that makes them special
- Detailed listings of restaurants, hotels, shops and nightlife
- Practical information

In addition, easy-to-read side panels provide fascinating extra facts and snippets, highlights of places to visit and invaluable practical advice.

CROSS-REFERENCES

To help you make the most of your visit, cross-references, indicated by ▶ show you where to find additional information about a place or subject.

MAPS

The fold-out map in the wallet at the back of the book is a large-scale map of Malta & Gozo.

The island maps found on the inside front and back covers of the book itself are for quick reference. They show the Top 25 Sights, described on pages 24–48, which are clearly plotted by number (**1**–**25**, not page number) in alphabetical order.

PRICES

Where appropriate, an indication of the cost of an establishment is given by £ signs: £££ denotes higher prices, ££ denotes average prices, while £ denotes lower charges.

MALTA & GOZO
life

A Personal View

Am I just another invader, arriving at Luqa airport with my suntan lotion and travel guide, to add to the catalogue of intruders from ancient times to World War II? Unlike the Arabs, Carthaginians, Romans and Europeans of the past, however, my visit is not unbidden. For the Maltese are now free to turn away gate-crashers, and visitors are welcomed as temporary guests who do not arrive to conquer but to enjoy and appreciate the delights of a small group of islands in the middle of the Mediterranean.

First impressions always linger in the mind and returning to Malta and Gozo never fails to bring them back, though each visit adds a sharper focus and another detail. Luqa airport is just another modern airport, anonymous and streamlined, but once outside, beginning with views through the window of a taxi, it is the quality of the light and the colours of the landscape that arrest the mind. What is striking are the honey-coloured walls of the modest sandstone houses, built on parched, ochre-coloured soil that shines under the unrelenting sun. The taxi ride invariably ends somewhere within sight of the sea and then one is struck by the intensity of the deep turquoise water and the brightly painted *luzzu* bobbing gently in the harbours.

Malta's coastline

The lucent sea and the ever-present sun alone would tempt many a visitor back to Malta and Gozo, more so now than ever before in view of the increasing pollution of so much of the Mediterranean's coastlines. And while the rest of Europe is still only thinking about shrugging off winter, the scent of citrus groves is in the wind and soon wildflowers begin to dot the fields, and bougainvillea and oleander grace the window boxes of people's homes. It is time for some fresh Mediterranean food served alfresco but in the shade – with a glass of wine.

The cultural landscape is as beguiling as the physical one, even in little ways like the endearingly ancient cars and buses that each carry their own little shrine – perhaps reflecting the sometimes perilous driving conditions – the archaic red telephone boxes, and families enjoying a leisurely evening stroll or *passeggiata*. The smaller and more verdant Gozo and minute Comino enhance even further the feeling of a place apart. Once you relax into a pace of life that is full of vitality, but a few steps back in time, the engaging affability of the Maltese people can be experienced at first hand.

On reflection, what seems to become the most remarkable aspect of Maltese life is the simple fact that the island's culture remains so distinctively its own. The enduring legacy of the Maltese language is testimony to this, even though just about everyone you meet is able to speak English fluently. There is also the pride invested in the country's past, from prehistoric monuments built 1,000 years before the pyramids to the awesome defensive works of the Knights of Malta. The Knights were the invaders, not you and me.

Luzzus *in Marsaxlokk harbour*

Many of Malta's colourful buses carry religious shrines

Malta in Figures

PEOPLE

- Some 330,000 Maltese live on the island of Malta and 26,000 (calling themselves Gozitans) live on the island of Gozo.
- Malta ranks fourth in the world in terms of population density.
- An estimated 300,000 Australians are of Maltese origin. Worldwide the figure is put at over 1 million.
- Most Maltese are Roman Catholics. The Catholic influence accounts for the fact that there are no divorces in Malta, abortion is illegal, and local religious festivals erupt with colour and celebration.

GOVERNMENT

- Malta is a constitutional republic whose members of parliament are elected every five years by universal suffrage.

SIZE

- Malta's longest distance from the southeast to the northwest is 27km and the widest point from east to west is 14km.
- Gozo is 14km long and 7km at its widest.

LANGUAGES

- Maltese and English are the official languages. Italian is widely spoken, German to a lesser extent.
- The Arab influence shows itself in the language, Maltese, 70 per cent of which is Arabic in origin.

WEATHER

- Temperatures in the summer can reach 30°C; lows of the year, around 14°C, occur in January and February.
- On average, the islands have six months of interrupted sunshine each year, between April and September.

Right: a historical map of Valletta clearly showing the fortifications
Opposite: two citizens of Rabat deep in conversation

People of Malta

For such a small island, Malta's geographical position meant that it was destined to play a memorable role in world events, notably during the centuries under the Knights of Malta and in World War II.

Politics

Dom Mintoff (1916–), a controversial and charismatic figure, dominated Maltese, and sometimes British politics for 30 years. From a poor family, he attended university in Malta and won a scholarship to Oxford. He joined the post-war, pro-British Labour Party of Malta. In 1955 he became Prime Minister and proposed the full integration of Malta into the United Kingdom, but Britain refused. Mintoff immediately changed his policy to one of full independence. He returned to power from 1971 to 1984 and in 1996 was re-elected as a Member of Parliament.

Art

Caravaggio (1571–1610), the greatest Italian painter of the 17th century, left his mark on the island after only a few months' stay here. He was notorious for his violent temper and, unusually, used common people as models for his paintings of saints. Wanted for murder in Rome, he accepted a commission from the Order in 1607 and painted *The Beheading of St John the Baptist*. He became a Knight, completed three more paintings, but became involved in a fight and was expelled from the order. He escaped from gaol and continued his short but colourful life elsewhere.

Among other famous artists to visit Malta over the centuries were the Spanish Mateo Perez d'Aleccio (1547–99), Italian Mattia Preti (1616–99) and the Frenchman Antoine de Favray (1706–98). Among the Maltese were the sculptor Melchiorre Gafa (1635–67), Francesco Zahra (1710–73), Guiseppe Cali (1846–1930) and Antonio Sciortino (1879–1947).

THE KNIGHTS OF MALTA

The wealth of both the Order of St John and the Knights themselves attracted artists to the island with which the Order will be for ever associated. This ensured the presence of outstanding works of art and architecture, and formidable defences.

The Knights Hospitallers of the Order of St John of Jerusalem was a religious order founded in Jerusalem in the 11th century. After the capture of Jerusalem by the Muslims in 1187, the Order moved to Rhodes but this, too, proved temporary. In 1530 the emperor of the Holy Roman Empire gave them the Maltese islands. The Grand Master, Jean Parisot de la Valette, made it their permanent home and prevented Suleyman from conquering Malta in the Great Siege of 1565.

A Chronology

5500–4100 BC	The Neolithic Age, when Sicilian colonists inhabit the islands. Skorba temples are built.
4100–2500 BC	The 'Copper Age', when the temples at Ġgantija, Tarxien and the Hypogeum at Ħal-Safflieni are built. Abruptly ends around 2500 BC.
2500–800 BC	The Bronze Age. Information about the period comes from the Tarxien Cemetery. Villages are fortified and the mysterious cart ruts at Għar il-Kibr appear.
c600 BC	Dominated by the Carthaginian trading empire. Phoenician colonists trade with Greece, build temples to the Phoenician gods, strike their own coins and organise complex rock tomb burials.
257 BC	A Roman force invades during the Punic Wars (Romans against Carthaginians) and many settlements are totally devastated.
218 BC	Malta is incorporated into the Roman empire. Elaborate catacomb burials become common. Punic temples are elaborated and Romanised villas appear in rural areas. Roman towns start to develop.
AD 60	St Paul, shipwrecked, converts the Roman governor to Christianity.
500–870	Byzantine empire now in control.
870–1090	Under Arab rule.
1090–1530	Colonised by succession of European powers: the Normans, Germans, French and Spanish.
1429	Sacked by Muslims.
1530	Charles V of Spain gives islands in perpetuity to the Knights Hospitallers of the Order of St John of Jerusalem.
1565	The Great Siege.

1566	The city of Valletta is founded.
1614	A second Turkish invasion is repelled.
1600s	A series of forts and towers is built around the coast, but no further Turkish invasions occur.
1700s	The Order of St John of Jerusalem declines as a fighting force, turning to trade.
1798	Napoleon invades. The Knights are ejected, never to return. Wholesale looting of churches. The Maltese call on the British for assistance.
1800	The French surrender and the British occupy the islands.
1814	The Treaty of Paris makes Malta a British Crown Colony.
1914–18	In World War I, Malta becomes 'Nurse of the Mediterranean'.
1942	World War II makes Malta a strategic target, bringing great hardship. On 15 April, the people and the island of Malta are awarded the George Cross for gallantry, by King George VI. In April alone, over 6,000 tonnes of bombs fall.
1962	State of Malta is created.
1964	Malta achieves independence within the Commonwealth.
1971	The Labour Party led by Dom Mintoff, elected.
1974	Malta becomes a Republic and remains in the Commonwealth.
1998	Snap election leads to a Nationalist government. Application for EU membership is renewed.
2004	Malta becomes a member of the EU.

Best of Malta

If you have only a short time to visit Malta & Gozo, or would like to get a really complete picture of the islands, here are some suggestions for activities and places that shouldn't be missed:

- See The Malta Experience audio-visual show (➤ 78) in Valletta for an enjoyable dip into history, covering 7,000 years in 50 minutes.
- Go to a *festa*, the Maltese village festival, for the fun and vitality, the colour and the sound effects (➤ 22).
- Enjoy Maltese food by tucking into *pastizzi* (➤ 65) with your mid-morning drink, and have at least one picnic with fresh bread, bought before 11AM, and peppered cheese from Gozo.
- Spend more than a day in Gozo because the pleasure of being there lies in its unhurried pace and a quick visit will fail to do justice to its many charms (➤ 18–19, 20).
- Visit St John's Co-Cathedral in Valletta (➤ 43) and see the Caravaggio paintings. The Italian painter came to Malta in 1607 and stayed only 14 months before escaping from prison for an unknown crime (➤ 9).
- See Mdina, the ancient capital, walled by the Arabs and separated from the suburbs which became Rabat. History stares back at you from the walls (➤ 37).

Above: girls shelter from the sun in Qrendi
Below: flags to celebrate Floriana Festival

- Visit at least one of the prehistoric sites: The Hypogeum (➤ 34) is the most informative. All bear testimony to Colin Renfrew's claim in *Before Civilization* that 'the great temples of Malta and Gozo lay claim to be the world's most impressive prehistoric monuments'.
- Go for a walk around Valletta, visiting a church here, a museum or art gallery there, forts and gardens (➤ 48).
- Buy some Maltese glass or Maltese lace, both artistic and affordable examples of local handicrafts (➤ 75–76).
- Take a cruise around the Grand Harbour, a magnificent and truly formidable sight that sparks the imagination (➤ 32).

MALTA & GOZO
how to organise your time

A Walk Around Floriana

To see Floriana and combine it with an interesting, pleasing stroll, begin at the Phoenicia Hotel, on Il-Mall.

INFORMATION

Distance 2km
Time 1 hour
Start/end point Phoenicia Hotel
✉ Il-Mall
☎ 21225241
🍴 Phoenicia Hotel (£££)

With your back to the Phoenicia Hotel's entrance, turn right and walk down to the Independence Monument in the middle of the road. The entrance to the Maglio Gardens is immediately behind the statue.

Enter the park, which was designed by a Grand Master as a place for young knights to exercise by playing a ball game in a large, narrow structure, since demolished. The shaded pathway is dotted with busts of various Maltese dignitaries. Over to the left you can clearly see the notable flat caps of the more than 70 subterranean granary silos in the huge square in front of St Publius Church (► 28).

At the end of the park's walkway exit on the left side to view Sarria Church on the other side of the road.

Enter Argotti Botanical Gardens by the side of the water tower. The gardens, dating back to the late 18th century, are well-maintained and there are several species of cacti, and exotic trees to admire.

At the end of the walkway there is a good view from the balcony of the suburbs, stretching across to Marsamxett Harbour.

Retrace your steps to the park's entrance and cross the road to the Sarria Church. Then follow the road down to the right until it meets the main road at a junction with a statue of a decrepit-looking lion gracing a fountain.

Turn left and walk up the main road towards Valletta, past shops and the American Consular office, to a roundabout. Keep to the left and the Phoenicia Hotel will be seen again on the other side of the car park.

Floriana's tree-lined gardens contain many statues

A Drive in West & Southwest Malta

This is a chance to explore another side of Malta.

From Valletta, drive to Ċirkewwa on the Gozo side of the isolated Marfa Peninsula. From Ċirkewwa follow the road back to Valletta until a right turn is signposted for Golden Bay and Manikata. On the road to Manikata a vista of sea suddenly appears and after 3km turn right at the unsignposted T-junction for Golden Bay.

Detour to Golden Bay (► 30), a popular family beach. After a quick swim or lie in the sun, carry on.

After less than 1km, at another T-junction, turn right and then straight on for Għajn Tuffieħa (► 30). Return to the main road and turn right, looking for a small sign on the right after 1.5km for the Roman Baths (► 30). After another 0.5km a detour may be made to Mġarr.

Look at the 'Egg Church' and perhaps make a stop here and have lunch – the return journey is under 2km – the main road goes on to Żebbieħ and the Skorba Temples.

From Żebbieħ head for Mdina (► 37) and then follow the signs for the Dingli Cliffs (► 59). Turn left at the coast, keeping the Mediterranean on your right until the road swings inland.

After 1.5km take the left turn at the roundabout, signposted for Rabat, and look for an unmarked crossroads with a church on the left. A left turn at this junction leads to Verdala Palace (► 55).

Stop for a tour of this cool palace if open.

Just 1km after the Palace the first turn left leads to Buskett Gardens (► 59), a sign points the way on to Clapham Junction (► 59).

Stretch your legs, and let yourself become absorbed in the mystery of the cart ruts. Then take the main road to Rabat.

INFORMATION

Distance 20km
Time 4–6 hours depending on visits to places of interest
Start point Ċirkewwa
End point Rabat & Mdina
✉ Magar, next to the church
☎ 21573235
🍴 Charles il-Barri (£–££)

Below: Dingli Cliffs

Verdala Palace was built as a summer residence by a Grand Master

15

A Walk Around Mdina

INFORMATION

Distance 1km

Time 2–4 hours, depending on visits

Start/end point Mdina Gate

🚌 80, 81, 83, 84, 86 from Valletta, 65 from Sliema

🍴 Fontanella Café (£)

✉ 1 Bastion Street

☎ 21454264

The walk begins at the Mdina Gate and immediately after passing through the gate, the Mdina Dungeons (► 56), a gruesome museum, is on the right. Next door is the Palazzo Vilhena and the National Museum of Natural History (► 53).

Take the first left and stay on this street, Triq Villegaignon, immediately passing Inguanez Street, which leads to the Bacchus restaurant (► 65), and then passing another left leading to the Mdina Experience (► 78). A little way beyond, Caffé Medina brings you into Pjazza San Pawl, St Paul's Square, with a large church bearing two clocks (one of which tells the correct time; the other is there to confuse the devil). Continue along Triq Villegaignon, past a leathercraft shop, and turn left into the narrow St Peter's Street. At the bottom, turn right into Magazine Street.

Walking along Magazine Street, you will pass the Knights of Malta exhibition, perhaps the least engaging of the various multimedia shows on offer in Mdina, but with a neat little café. There are views from the terrace here and more alfresco places up ahead which are worth a stop.

After passing a second tea garden, walk into Bastion Square where there are views from the ramparts and places to enjoy a rest and a drink. Take the first right turning into the Triq Villegaignon.

Here, at the top end of the Triq Villegaignon, you first pass Palazzo Falzon (► 55) and then Medieval Times, with its Palazzo Notabile eatery serving pizza and pasta.

The walk starts and ends at the Mdina gate

Take the first left after Palazzo Notabile into the narrow St Roque Street and at the T-junction, at the bottom of the street, go left into Bastion Street and pass the entrance to Fontanella Café. Go left, take the first left into Our Savior Street and follow this street until, turning left at the T-junction, you are back on Triq Villegaignon which leads back to the starting point.

A Drive Around the North Coast

The North Coast was where St Paul was shipwrecked and where the Turks and later Napoleon landed.

Follow Tower Road in Sliema in the direction of St Julian's, following the signs for St Paul's Bay and Mellieħa. Once outside the town the first stopping point is the unsignposted village of Għargħur (➤ 50).

To reach it, turn left at the turning for Madliena which is signposted (if you pass Splash Park you have gone too far) and follow the winding road up to Għargħur.

Soak up the atmosphere of this ancient elevated village with fine views and enjoy a mid-morning drink in the tiny King George VI bar.

Retrace your route to the main road, turn left to continue west towards St Paul's Bay.

The road hugs the coast as far as Salina Bay before reaching Buġibba and St Paul's Bay. A walk along the promenade in St Paul's should give you an appetite for lunch. Don't miss Għajn Razul (Apostle's Fountain) where St Paul is said to have baptized the first Maltese.

After lunch drive the short distance further west to Mellieħa (➤ 38), stopping perhaps at the island's largest sandy beach which is just 2km north of the town, descending the ridge. From the beach continue on to the northwest corner of Malta, the Marfa Ridge, and photogenic Ċirkewwa, from where the ferries depart for Gozo.

There are a number of small beaches near here which, outside weekends, attract few visitors.

From Ċirkewwa head back to Mellieħa and turn right at the main roundabout to head south to Għajn Tuffieħa (➤ 30). From here take the main road to Żebbieħ, Mosta and Naxxar (➤ 50–51). From Naxxar it is a short distance back to Sliema.

INFORMATION

Distance 40km
Time 6–8 hours
Start/end point Sliema
🍴 Gillieru Restaurant, St
Paul's Bay (££–£££)
☎ 21573480

Middle: St Paul's Bay
Above: Armier Bay
Beach, Marfa Ridge

17

A Walk Around Gozo

For a walk in southern Gozo, drive or take a bus to Sannat, the most southerly village, close to the Ta'Cenc cliffs.

INFORMATION

Distance 4km
Time 2 hours
Start point Sannat
End point Just north of Mġarr ix-Xini

🚌 42, 43
🍴 Chip and Dale Bar (£)
✉ Town Square, Victoria
☎ 21560506

At the southern end of Sannat follow the sign-posted left turnings to Ta'Cenc/Dolmen Cliffs. If driving, park where the last sign points left; next to an advert for Il-Girma restaurant. You will find a fine view of Xewkija's domed church, The Rotunda (► 39), dominating the plain on your left. There is also a superb view of Victoria's acropolis, the Citadel.

You arrive at a crossroad of sorts (the roads are currently being surfaced) where you turn left, rather than straight on which leads down to the sea and a small private beach belonging to a hotel. The road you are on has a view of Comino and the western coastline of Malta up ahead in the distance, while all around is Gozo's barren landscape of limestone and scrubland. In this vicinity there are cart ruts (► 59) and neolithic burial mounds, but they are not signposted and it takes a bit of luck to stumble across them.

After less than 1km the road heads downhill for 600m; turn to the left and follow the road; after about 0.5km the trail winds down to the inlet of Mġarr ix-Xini.

This is the perfect place for a rest and ideal for a picnic, and there is also the enticing prospect of a swim in the cool safe water.

From Mġarr ix-Xini it is 1.5km uphill along a surfaced road to a T-junction where the road to the right goes to Xewkija and the left road is signposted to Victoria. (Along this road to the left there is a bus stop with a service that will take you back to Victoria.)

Top: Xewkija Rotunda Church
Above: view of the Citadel's walls

18

A Drive Around Gozo

The northern coast of Gozo can be breezy and was once desolate – a place of legends.

After disembarking the ferry at Mġarr follow the signposted road to the right for Nadur. The uphill road leads to a T-junction; take the right turn for Qala, less than 1km away. Exposed Qala has remnants of windmills, sun-baked dwellings and dusty roads with a Moorish feel.

Continue straight past the church. Go left at the T-junction, signposted for Nadur.

At Nadur there is a maritime museum with exhibits from sailing ships and battleships of World War II.

Leave Nadur on the road to Victoria and after 1.5km take the right turn at the junction for Xagħra. Follow the signs for Xagħra and follow the road as it climbs uphill with a sign on the right for Ġgantija (► 29). Stay on the road to Xagħra after Ġgantija but take the second turning on the right, passing down the side of the church (cafés and bars in the square) and bearing left at the signposted junctions for Marsalforn.

There is a good view of Marsalforn as you enter the village through this back door approach. Stop here for lunch and a walk.

Take the road to Victoria from Marsalforn but turn right at the main junction before entering Victoria and look for the sign to Ta'Pinu.

The basilica at Ta'Pinu, a centre of pilgrimage for both Gozitans and Maltese, is noted for its mysterious voices and miraculous cures.

After the short detour to Ta'Pinu, return to the main road and take the signposted left turn for Dwejra. At St Lawrenz bear left in front of the church; the Azure Window and Fungus Rock is 1km (► 24).

INFORMATION

Distance 12km
Time 2–5 hours depending on visits
Start point Mġarr ferry terminal
End point Dwerja
🍴 Il-Kartell (£–££)
✉ Waterfront in Marsalforn
☎ 21556918

Kelinu Grima Maritime Museum
✉ Parish Priest Street, Nadur
☎ 21565226
🕐 Mon–Sat 9–4:45 (except public holidays)

The drive passes through countryside like this near Xagħra

19

Finding Peace & Quiet

Coming directly from the airport to the resorts of Buġibba or St Julian's one could be forgiven for thinking there is no peace and quiet in Malta. Fortunately – because of the islands of Gozo and Comino – it is easy to correct this fallacy.

BIRDWATCHING

Seabirds may be spotted from the clifftops of Gozo and the Marfa Peninsula on Malta, and the islands' strategic position as a resting station has long been appreciated by migrant species passing between northern Europe and Africa. The Ghadira Nature Reserve (☎ 21347646) is worth visiting for its bird life. Admission is free and the reserve is open at weekends (closed for lunch) between November and May. Buses 44, 645 or 48 will take you there.

GOZO'S APPEAL

Gozo may have one of the best discos and one of the best top class hotels in Malta (► 73), but the characteristic appeal of the place is not hedonistic. Given its small size one can cycle or walk anywhere along quiet country roads passing small family farms or following the rugged coastline along clifftop paths. Apart from the walk around Gozo (► 18), there are a number of other rewarding walks on the island and a useful leaflet with a map of walks is available from the Gozo Tourist Office.

THE BLUE LAGOON

The island of Comino (► 27) is inundated with boatloads of day visitors but it is the Blue Lagoon

that is the focus of interest and, given the absence of cars and the small distances (hardly more than a kilometre in any direction), one may escape from people. It helps to be here in spring when flowers give joyful relief to the barren landscape. It is even better to stay the night, because after sunset or early in the morning you will have Comino to yourself.

Banyan trees offer shade in San Anton Gardens

PARKS AND GARDENS

On Malta itself there are numerous opportunities to escape the hustle and bustle. The tourist office has a useful brochure listing and describing the various parks and gardens where one can seek solace, shade and enjoy a picnic far away from the fast-food restaurants and the crowds. One of the most attractive and larger parks is the San Anton Gardens (▶ 50) where some of the sub-tropical trees are labelled, including a splendid pair of wide-spreading Banyan trees, *Ficus benghalensis*, on the main path, and there is a small aviary to amuse young children.

AROUND MALTA

Malta's capital, Valletta, is remarkably quiet and peaceful at night. Apart from a few restaurants and bars there is very little open after 7PM. A stroll up Triq Marsamxett to Fort St Elmo and down the other side past the Lower Barracca Gardens is relaxing aand offers fine views of Marsamxett Harbour and Grand Harbour (▶ 32).

The clifftop landscape in the southwest of Malta offers some of the best opportunities for getting away on your own and, from April to June or during September and October, is a good place for bird watching. A recommended short walk is south from the village of Dingli (▶ 59) to the coast and then northwest along the ridge to Il-Qaws. With a good map one could thread one's way back to Rabat from here or return to Dingli for a bus.

WILD FLOWERS

The countryside often seems barren and sun-baked but suddenly between February and May it becomes surprisingly verdant, and crocuses, tulips and fritillarias shower the fields with colour. There are over 600 species of wild flowers. Gozo is always greener because of its clay soil and slightly hillier landscape.

From Lower Barracca Gardens you can see the Seige Bell Memorial dedicated to the men who died in the convoys of 1940–43

What's On

Public Holidays

Between May and October every town and village celebrates the feast day (*festa*) of its patron saint.

JANUARY

New Year's Day (1 Jan).

FEBRUARY

Feast of St Paul's Shipwreck (10 Feb): Valletta.

MARCH

Freedom Day (31 Mar).

MARCH/APRIL

Holy Week: Processions are held in various villages and towns around Malta and Gozo. Good Friday pageants are held in 14 different towns and villages featuring a number of life-sized statues depicting religious scenes. There will also be men and women in period costume personifying biblical characters. Many places of entertainment are closed but cinemas and cafés remain open.

MAY

Worker's Day (1 May).

JUNE

Feast of St Peter and Paul (29 Jun): parish *festa* in Nadur (Gozo).

AUGUST

Feast of the Assumption: Parish *festas* in Attard, Għaxaq, Gudja, Mġarr, Mosta, Mqabba, Qrendi, Victoria Cathedral (Gozo).

SEPTEMBER

Victory Day (8 Sep).
Independence Day (21 Sep).

DECEMBER

Feast of the Immaculate Conception (8 Dec).
Republic Day (13 Dec).
Christmas Day (25 Dec).

FESTAS

From the food stalls to the colourful parades and the carnival atmosphere, eveyone will enjoy a *festa*. The fireworks displays are especially good. Details are listed in the *Malta Independent*.

VICTORY DAY

A commemorative ceremony is held in Valletta to celebrate the lifting of the 1565 siege against the Turks, the capitulation of the French in 1880 and the end of the siege of the Axis powers in 1943. A colourful and keenly contested boat race is held in the Grand Harbour (8 Sep).

MALTA & GOZO's
top 25 sights

The sights are shown on the maps on the inside front cover and inside back cover, numbered **1**–**25** alphabetically

23

The Azure Window and Fungus Rock

INFORMATION

➕ A4

✉ 2km west of San Lawrenz

🍴 Drinks and snacks (£) available in the car park area

🚌 91 from Victoria

♿ None

💷 Inexpensive

Top: Azure Window
Above: Dwerja Point at Azure Window

An arch in the rock that forms a natural window on the deep blue sea; and, offshore, a huge outcrop of rock with a history.

The road west from San Lawrenz descends towards Dwejra Point through a landscape that even by Gozo's standards would seem especially desiccated were it not for the penetrating blueness of the Mediterranean offering a comforting contrast with the arid-looking coastline. Over the millennia, wind and water have eroded the soft rock to form a number of geological points of interest. What Gozitans call Tieqa Zerqa, the Azure Window, is a short walk from the car park at the end of the road and this natural phenomenon encapsulates the contrast with a beauty of its own. The natural arch of the rock has firm and solid sides but the top, an increasingly thin and fragile layer of fossilized sea creatures, is best not walked over.

The nearby, 20m-high outcrop called Fungus Rock acquired its name because the rock's fungus-like vegetation, a plant known as the Maltese sponge (*Cynomorium coccineum*), was believed to be a natural medicine that acted as a blood clotting agent as well as being a supposed remedy for dysentery. The Knights of Malta cornered the market for this valuable product by outlawing its collection except for their own use. They built a guard tower and devised a primitive rope and pulley system to access the rock; a futile endeavour in the light of subsequent research that showed the fungus possessed no medicinal qualities.

The geology of this western end of Gozo has also created Il-Qawra, the Inland Sea, a land-locked sea-water pool but with a natural tunnel in the rock that allows in the sea water. Boat trips are available for passage into the salt-water lagoon through the tunnel and the trips take in some sightseeing along the coast.

Blue Grotto

The Blue Grotto experience is a very popular half-hour boat trip that skirts the coast in colourfully painted boats from the fishing village of Wied-iz.

It requires a boat ride to appreciate the cave-filled, craggy geography of Malta's southern coastline and there is no more enjoyable way of achieving this than by way of a Blue Grotto boat trip.

The boats used are open-air, eight-seaters with outboard motors, so suitable clothing is the order of the day, and a camera will not go amiss. The popularity of these trips with tour coaches can mean waiting in a queue, so try to arrive early in the morning, though some of the boatmen claim early afternoon is the ideal time to enjoy the trip.

If arriving in your own transport, the views along the road from Zurrieq to the narrow fjord of Wied iz-Zurrieq are an attraction in their own right. Bear in mind, too, that if the sky is overcast by clouds you will miss much of the play of light that adds so much to the quality of the boat ride experience.

There are a number of sea caves to see on the trip out, but it is the largest of the caves that is named the Blue Grotto. The Maltese name, That il-Hnejja, means beneath the arch and the appropriateness of this description becomes apparent when you view the massive arched rock at the entrance to the cave. Equally appropriate, though, is the name that the British gave to That il-Hnejja – the Blue Grotto – for a blue algae in the water adds a beautiful coloured sheen to the crystal clear surface of the sea.

INFORMATION

➕ D4
✉ Wied-iz-Zurrieq, 3km southwest of Zurrieq
🕐 Daily 8–4
🍴 Cafés (£) between the car park and the sea
🚌 38, 138
♿ None
💷 Inexpensive
↔ Ħaġar Qim & Mnajdra (► 33), Qrendi (► 51)

Blue Grotto was named for the colour created by blue algae in the water

25

Church of St Paul's Shipwreck

INFORMATION

➕ IBC

✉ Triq San Pawl (St Paul's Street)

☎ 21236013

🕐 Mon–Sun 9:30–11:45. No admission when mass is celebrated

🍴 Cafés and restaurants (£) within walking distance

♿ None

✋ Free

↔ Bibliotheca (➤ 59)

A small baroque church, easily missed and often nearly empty, but full of reminders of St Paul's historic, and accidental, visit to the island

With the justifiably much-vaunted St John's Co-Cathedral stealing all the thunder as far as Valletta's churches go, the Church of St Paul's Shipwreck is often skipped past by visitors, sometimes almost literally because it is easy to walk down St Paul's Street and pass by the church unknowingly. This is mainly because of its narrow dimensions, due presumably to the need to accommodate the building into a congested area of the city centre. Thought to have been designed by Gerolamo Cassar in the 16th century, although this has not been clearly established, the edifice underwent extensive modifications and in the process gained a number of adornments that are now its chief attractions. The façade of the church dates back to the end of the 19th century.

The church was built to commemorate St Paul's arrival on the island in AD60 when he was shipwrecked on his way to face trial in Rome. the gilded wooden statue of the saint that stands to the left of the church altar is removed once a year, on the saint's feast day on 10th February, and a procession starts outside the church under a shower of confetti. The church interior is home to a tiny shrine said to contain a part of St Paul's wrist bone, but you will strain your eyes trying to make it out because you can't get very close to the display. Another supposed relic is a section of the column on which St Paul was beheaded in Rome. More clearly visible are ceiling frescoes and a splendid altar painting by the Florentine artist Paladini depicting the famous shipwreck.

The attractive façade of The Church of St Paul's Shipwreck

Comino

Comino, a virtually uninhabited island, sits between Malta and Gozo. There are no cars or roads and only one hotel that opens for the summer.

INFORMATION

- C4
- Comino Hotel (££)
- From Malta and Gozo
- None

This tiny island, only 2.5km by 2km, makes a wonderful location for a peaceful retreat.

The island's history is unremarkable for it seems that only pirates were attracted to its coves and creeks and in 1618 a promontory fort, Comino Tower, was built on Comino's west side.

Unless resident at the hotel, visitors come for a day trip to enjoy the crystal-clear turquoise water or slow walks in the fresh air along vehicle-free pathways (and it is impossible to get lost!). The whole island is a wildlife sanctuary but botanically, the island is not as interesting as might be hoped, and it is not easy to find the cumin plant (*kemmuna*) from which the island receives its name. If staying on the island, there are excellent diving possibilities and even daytrippers can enjoy snorkelling if they bring their own gear.

The only significant beach area is the Blue Lagoon, formed by a channel that separates sun-baked and barren Comino from the islet of Cominotto, and only the density of bathers detracts from the intrinsic beauty of this lagoon with its fine white sand. It is essential to arrive on Comino as early as possible, especially if you want to enjoy the Blue Lagoon. Be sure to bring protective clothing, cold drinks and a picnic, although food and drinks are available at the hotel.

Comino's Blue Lagoon attracts swimmers to the island

Floriana

INFORMATION

✚ E3

✉ To the immediate south of Valletta, a few minutes walk from the city's bus terminal

🕐 St Publius Church is open for services on Saturday evening and Sunday morning. Sarria Church has a Sunday morning service at 10:30

🍽 Cafés and restaurants (£–££) within walking distance in Valletta

♿ Good

↔ Valletta (➤ 48)

This pleasant suburb of Valletta was largely rebuilt after World War II, but there are some notable reminders of the past.

Best explored on foot, a pleasant afternoon can be spent exploring Floriana (➤ 14).

Paolo Floriani was an Italian military engineer sent by the Pope in 1634 to further strengthen Valletta by a secondary defence system (Floriana Lines) outside the city.

The largest structure is St Publius Church, which was finally completed in 1792, nearly 40 years after the first stone was laid, while its classical portico is a late 19th-century addition. The entire edifice was largely rebuilt after extensive damage during World War II. The vast open space in front of the church is distinguished by a number of large stone caps which are the protruding lids to over 70 granary pits. The pits were dug in the 17th century to store food safely and they were used again from 1941 to 1943 when Malta was once more under siege.

One of the most singular churches in Malta is the circular and compact Sarria Church, built in 1676 to fulfill a vow that was made by the Order of St John at the height of a terrible plague earlier in the year. Opposite the church is the Wignacourt Water Tower, an elaborate fountain that was constructed under Grand Master Wignacourt in 1615, part of an aqueduct system built to supply Valletta with water from the hills around Mdina. The nearby Argotti Botanical Gardens, with exotic trees and rare cacti, offer an escape from the traffic that pours through Floriana. So too does Maglio Gardens, a cultured strip of garden and tree-lined walkway that stretches from the Argotti Gardens back towards Valletta.

A statue in Floriana's Maglio Gardens offers a perch for passing birds

Ġgantija

Immense bare rock, curious features and primitive attempts at decoration are the stunning signs of a 5,000-year-old technology and culture.

Dating back to 3500–3000 BC, Malta's 'Copper Age', the temples at Ġgantija (pronounced Jagan-Teeya) on Gozo are thought to be the world's oldest free-standing monuments. The site is an artificial plateau with a sweeping panorama. Primitive in structure, it is its size which creates a sense of wonder, particularly the outer walls. According to legend, they were built by a female giant. The coralline limestone blocks of the outer wall, some weighing as much as 20 tonnes, were quarried from the hill on the other side of the valley and probably rolled and dragged over using the rounded stones that lie scattered in front of the temples. The blocks were stood upright by building earth ramps, and large vertical supporting slabs support smaller rectangular blocks.

The temples themselves tell us something about the organisation and religion of the complex society that built these structures. Two buildings, one larger and older than the other, seem to have been places of worship to a fertility goddess. It has even been suggested that the shape of the structures themselves represent the body of the goddess (head and breasts). Inside the smaller structure, about 200 years younger, stone female figures were found, although these belong to a later date than the construction of the buildings. In the doorway of the larger structure are hinge holes used to support doors which would once have separated worshippers from the priests who were in the outer and central inner temples. Inside, two holes in the floor are thought to be libation holes where the blood of the sacrificed was poured. In the centre of the building, which was once 6m high with a domed roof, a large triangular stone and another one carved into the shape of a phallus were found.

INFORMATION

➕ B4

✉ Ġgantija, near Xagħra, Gozo

☎ 21553194

🕐 1 Oct–31 Mar, Mon–Sat 8:30–4:30, Sun 8:30–3; 1 Apr–15 Jun, Mon–Sat 8:30–6:30, Sun 8:30–3; 16 Jun–15 Sep, Mon–Sat 8:30–7, Sun 8:30–3; 16 Sep–30 Sep, Mon–Sat 8:30–6:30, Sun 8:30–3

🍴 Oleander (££, ➤ 69) or café (£) in Xagħra

🚌 64, 65 from Victoria

♿ Few

💶 Inexpensive

The huge ancient coralline limestone structures here are thought to represent the body of a goddess

29

Għajn Tuffieħa and Golden Bay

Two lovely, neighbouring, beaches with very different characters. A visit to both is worthwhile to experience the contrast.

The two sandy beaches of Għajn Tuffieħa and Golden Bay, separated by a small headland, have military associations. It was in Għajn Tuffieħa that the Turkish fleet gathered before beginning the Great Siege of 1565, and the British trained their naval forces in both bays during World War II.

Today, they attract mostly sun worshippers but the excavated Roman Baths near by reveal a shared concern with the serious pursuit of leisure. The baths belonged to a Roman villa, now largely disappeared but the baths were renovated by UNESCO in 1961 to show a complex that consisted of warm and cold baths, a hot-air room with underground heating and a separate small swimming pool.

Golden Bay boasts a broad sweep of sand backed by a café and tourist development on the hill above. It is often busy. Għajn Tuffeiħa, however, attracts far fewer people, possibly because it is accessed only by a steep staircase. Occasional northwest winds create dangerous currents in the deeper parts of both bays and a red warning flag indicates the need to remain in the shallow part of the water.

Golden Bay on Malta's north coast is a delight for sun-seekers

Gozo Citadel and Cathedral

The origins of this fortified enclave reach back to Gozo's early history under Roman and Arab occupation. There is plenty to see.

In 1551 Turkish raiders penetrated its defences and soon after this the Knights set about constructing sturdy bastions and ordering all Gozitans to spend their nights inside its walls – a policy that did not officially come to an end for almost 100 years. Now, the Citadel is virtually uninhabited at night, though by day there is a constant flow of travellers visiting the cathedral, the few craft shops and many museums.

The Folklore Museum is the favourite of many visitors with its down-to-earth collection of practical artefacts, including two splendid mills. The Archaeological Museum has an important collection of Roman remains and Gozitan antiquities and, if time is limited, this and the Folklore Museum are the two worth seeing. The Craft Centre has displays of local pottery, glass, wrought iron and lace which are not for sale but may whet your shopping appetite for the goods found inside the Citadel.

Many of the buildings inside the Citadel were destroyed by Dragut, in the seige of 1551, and in the earthquake of 1693, but the whole complex has been sympathetically restored and a walk around the ramparts offers terrific views while evoking a sense of Gozo's ancient past.

The entrance to the Citadel in Victoria leads into a piazza with broad steps occupying most of one side, which lead to the cathedral of the Assumption of Our Lady. The exterior is perfectly proportioned, as befits a building designed by Lorenzo Gafa, but there is no dome where Gafa intended one. Visual compensation is provided inside: the flat roof has the illusion of a dome painted onto it, this trompe l'oeil being an outstanding feature.

INFORMATION

➕ B4

Folklore Museum, Museum of Archaeology and Natural Science Museum
☎ 21230711
🕐 Mon–Sat 8:30–4:30, Sun 8:30–3. Craft Centre Apr–Sep, Mon–Sat 7:30–6:45; Oct–Mar, 7:15–4:45
🍽 Cafés and restaurants (£–££) within walking distance
♿ Few
💲 Inexpensive

Victoria Tourist Office
✉ Tigrija Palazz, Republic Street
☎ 21561419
🕐 Mon–Sat 9–11:30, 1–5, Sun 9–12:30

Gozo Cathedral
➕ B4
✉ The Citadel
☎ 21556087
🕐 Museum: Mon–Sat 10–1, 1:30–4:30
🍽 Cafés and restaurants (£–££) within walking distance
♿ Good
💲 Inexpensive

The vantage point of the Citadel is excellent for photographs of Gozo's countryside

Grand Harbour

INFORMATION

✚ E3

Sliema Marina

🕐 Tours leave from Sliema
Marina, check times

🍴 Lunch and dinner cruises
are available

🚌 60, 61, 62, 63, 64, 67, 68
from Valletta, 70 from
Buġibba, 65 from Rabat,
645 from Ċirkewwa, 652
from Golden Bay

ℹ Valletta–Sliema ferry
(☎ 21338981, 21343373)

Spread out like a living painting, several hundred years of history bake quietly in the Mediterranean sunshine.

The truly formidable ramparts are best viewed from one of the many boat trips which go out into the harbour for a day or half-day trip. However, if time does not allow for that there are several good viewing points from land, particularly from Upper Barracca Gardens (► 59). Boat tours generally leave from Sliema Marina passing Fort Manoel on the right and crossing Marsamxett Harbour, where the northern fortifications of Valletta can be seen. Grand Harbour itself is guarded by the two forts of Fort St Elmo and Fort Ricasoli, appearing as the tour passes briefly into open sea before turning west into the harbour. As you pass Fort St Elmo (► 54), damage done by the Italians in 1941 can still be seen.

Built as a fortress city and developed as a naval base and dockyard by the British, Valletta sits snugly between this harbour and Marsamxett. Looking up at the towering eastern shore of Valletta the wharves of the marina, with its 16th- and 17th-century buildings, can be seen, surmounted by the Sacra

Tour boats cruising the blue waters of the Grand Harbour offer an excellent view of Valletta's fortifications

Infermeria, Lower Barracca Gardens and Upper Barracca Gardens. Opposite Valletta's eastern defences are the fingers of land which make up Senglea and Vittoriosa. Between them can be seen the Cottonera Lines, a great 2-km inland defensive wall built in the 1670s. From the tips of these two points in 1565 the Knights of St John strung a chain to prevent the Turkish fleet of 200 vessels from entering Dockyard Creek, which was then the main harbour. Dominating the whole scene is Fort St Angelo (► 54).

Ħaġar Qim and Mnajdra

Over a thousand years before the pyramids, two temples were built on an evocative and spectacular site close to the sea.

The two temple complexes illustrate the ingenuity and complex social structure of a society that lived here for 3,000 years, then suddenly disappeared between 2500 and 1800 BC. This is megalithic architecture of a high order.

Ħaġar Qim ('Standing Stones'), first excavated in 1839, is a series of radiating oval rooms added on at various times to a trefoil structure. Holes around the entrance show where hinged doors once stood with bars to lock them shut. The stone is soft globigerina limestone which was easy to decorate, as can be seen in the pitted and spiral decoration, which accordingly has weathered badly. One stone here measures 7m by 3m.

Mnajdra, the second temple site, is a five-minute walk away in the direction of the sea but in a more sheltered spot. Made from a harder coralline limestone, it is far better preserved. The three temples share a common outer wall and presumably at one time shared a roof. There are the same patterns of pitted and spiral decorations, an outer temple with inner sanctuaries, carved recesses, trilithon door frames (two large pillars holding up a third block) and, in the second temple, an oracular window (through which the high priest or oracle might have spoken).

Both Ħaġar Qim and Mnajdra are thought to be expressions of a fertility-worshipping religion. Carved obese female figures have been found at both sites, as well as numerous other artefacts which can be seen in the Museum of Archaeology at Valletta (▶ 40).

The small islet to be seen out at sea is Filfa, just 1km in circumference.

INFORMATION

✚ D4

✉ 1.5km southwest of Qrendi

◷ 16 Jun–30 Sep, Mon–Sat 7:45–2; 1 Oct–15 Jun, Mon–Sat 8:15–5, Sun 8:15–4:15

🍴 Bar and restaurant (££) near the car park

🚌 38, 138

♿ Few

💲 Inexpensive

❓ Although Mnajdra is closed indefinitely, it is possible to see the site through the fence

Top: Mnajdra is fairly well preserved because it is made of coralline limestone
Below: These dressed globigerina limestone blocks at Ħaġar Qim date to around 2800BC

Hypogeum

➕ E3

✉ Burials Street, Paola

☎ 21825579

🕐 16 Jun–30 Sep, Mon–Sun tours 8:45, 9:45, 10:45, 11:45; 1 Oct–15 Jun, Mon–Sun tours 8:45, 9:45, 10:45, 11:45, 1:45, 2:45, 3:45 (last tour on Sun at 2:45)

🍴 Cafés and restaurants in Paola (£)

🚌 8, 11

♿ None

💷 Inexpensive

❓ Tickets for the tour should be purchased in advance. Booking a week ahead can be necessary at busy times as a maximum of ten people is allowed per group

🔁 Tarxien Temples (➤ 47)

This vast and complex underground carved temple, along with its catacombs, is unique to both Malta and Europe.

This underground burial place and temple covering an area of 799sq m was discovered in 1902 by workmen, who were laying the foundations of a house when they broke through the roof of the upper temple. Realising that building would stop if the authorities discovered its existence, they kept quiet about it, but three years later the news was out. Eventually, the site was excavated and was discovered to consist of three levels of catacombs, descending to 11m, the highest and oldest level being naturally occurring chambers while the two lower levels were carved out of the soft limestone. After a long period of renovation, the Hypogeum is once again open to the public.

A visit begins with a video show that places the Hypogeum in its historical context, followed by a guided tour of the three levels. The tour is informative and questions can be asked but, as the guide will tell you, there is a lot of educated conjecture when it comes to explaining the Hypogeum. The top level was in use c3000 BC as a burial ground. Descending by modern stairs to the middle level the visitor encounters carved pillars as well as spiral and hexagonal decorations, probably created around 2500 BC. The guide gives a possible explanation for the Oracle Chamber and points out parts of the walls still bearing traces of the red ochre that once provided a means of decoration. Visitors can see but not step down into the lowest level.

Besides human remains, statues, amulets, vases and other objects were found during excavation. Replicas of many of these can be seen in the exhibition area at the Hypogeum; the originals are in the Museum of Archaeology in Valletta.

The main chamber of the Hypogeum

Manoel Theatre

Whether it be a dramatic production, piano recital or orchestral concert, make sure you grab the opportunity to see a live performance if you can.

The Knights. who so much enjoyed dramatic performances in their auberges, commissioned this theatre which was opened in 1732.

After a long period of disuse, then conversion to a hostel for the homeless and later a cinema, this gem of a theatre was beautifully restored in 1960. The stalls area is tiny, as is the stage, but enclosing both are three tiers of ornately decorated boxes in soft green and gold and above them a gallery area from where a spectator could reach out and touch the gilded ceiling which has a solitary chandelier in its centre. If there is an opportunity to see any performance do not hesitate to book; the theatre season runs from October to May. Regardless of performances, the courtyard café is always worth a visit in its own right.

INFORMATION

➕ IBC
✉ Triq il-Teatru il-Qadim (Old Theatre Street)
☎ 21222618 (theatre), 21242977 (museum)
🕐 Guided tours Mon–Fri 10:30, 11:30, 4:30, Sat 11:30, 12:30
🍴 Café (£, ➤ 62)
♿ None
💲 Inexpensive
🔁 Palace of the Grand Masters (➤ 42), Bibliotheca (➤ 59)

Glowing lights illuminate the theatre's interior which was restored in 1960

35

Marsaskala

INFORMATION

- ✚ F3
- ✉ 9km southeast of Valletta
- 🍴 Cafés and restaurants (£–££) by the seafront
- 🚌 19, 20, 22
- ♿ Few
- ❓ Luzzo Cruises (➤ 79) run boat trips from Marsaskala to Gozo and Grand Harbour, and organise fishing trips

The postcard-pretty harbour of Marsaskala (also spelt Marsascala) witnessed the last Turkish assault on Malta in 1614.

Although the troops landed they were beaten back while heading inland and the Knights quickly built a mighty fort on the nearby headland to deter any future visits.

Today, a tourist infrastructure is developing quickly and Marsaskala welcomes visitors with open arms. Appropriately enough, part of the fort's location has been turned into the area's premier tourist hotel, the Jerma Palace Hotel. The village of Marsaskala has an agreeable setting by the water's edge with plenty of cafés and good seafood restaurants overlooking the bay and its pastel-coloured boats. In recent years the nightlife scene has become increasingly popular with visitors and Maltese alike. Between them, the bars and discos and an up-to-date cinema and restaurant complex appeal across the age range.

There is no beach, but nearby St Thomas Bay, 1km to the south, has sandy banks and shallow water. In summer it can seem too busy, but it is easy to escape the crowds by heading south along the coast

Marsaskala's pleasant waterfront in the fading light of day

towards Delimara Point. The road to St Thomas Bay from Marsaskala passes Mamo Tower, a 17th-century tower with an interesting cruciform design and just one room with a vaulted roof. It was privately built by a landowner to deter slave-collecting expeditions from North Africa dropping in to St Thomas Bay and abducting his peasants.

Mdina and Rabat

High ground away from the coast made Mdina a natural site for a defensively minded community. Bronze Age man was probably first to settle here.

The Phoenicians and Romans knew it respectively as Maleth and Melita while the Arabs built walls 19m high around the town they called Mdina, leaving the poorer people outside in an area that came to be known as Rabat. In the following centuries Mdina emerged as the island's capital and remained so until the Knights made Valletta the new capital in 1571.

Today, fortified medieval Mdina and Rabat should not be missed by any first-time visitor. Mdina's honey-coloured walls and narrow winding alleyways and Rabat's catacombs and Roman remains make any visit memorable.

Magazine Street and Greek's Gate

Magazine Street, so called because munitions were once stored here, borders the western side of Mdina and, unless a tour group has arrived, there is a surprising air of tranquillity to the place. There are many fine details to appreciate in the old dwellings, and photographers, if the light allows, enjoy trying to capture in close-up the brass knockers, the cut stone or the window mouldings.

Greek's Gate is named after a small number of Greeks who came to Malta with the Knights from Rhodes and settled in this corner of Mdina. The walls of Greek's Gate are very old, dating back to Arab times. Just north of Greek's Gate is another breach in the wall, made in the 19th century for those travelling to Mdina by train. The old train station, now a restaurant with the bar at what was the ticket office and the dining room in the waiting room (➤ 66), can be seen in the valley below.

INFORMATION

- ✚ C3
- ⏹ Cafés and restaurants (£–££) in Mdina and Rabat
- 🚌 80, 81, 83, 84 from Valletta, 65 from Sliema and Valletta
- ♿ Steep and narrow, uneven surfaces

Entering medieval Mdina through the Greek's Gate

Mellieħa

INFORMATION

➕ B1

✉ 23km west of Valletta

🍴 A good choice of cafés and restaurants (£–££)

🚌 43, 44, 45 (+50 in summer) from Valletta, 48 from Buġibba and Ċirkewwa, 645 from Sliema and Ċirkewwa

♿ Few

This place has always been a favourite destination with the Maltese, and is now becoming popular with visitors to the island.

Mellieħa's popular sandy beach – the largest in Malta – is 2km north of town. It attracted Turkish pirates which led to the village of Mellieħa, which is set on a spur, being deserted in the mid-16th century.

The town's present shape goes back to the 19th century when the steep main street, where houses cling to the rock, was laid out. Selmun Palace, a prominent castle with adjoining chapel, that dominates the area from its position up on the ridge, was built in the mid-18th century by Domenica Cathias. It was once owned by a charitable foundation which aimed to ransom Christian slaves who had been taken to the Barbary Coast. It is now a hotel.

The heritage prize, however, goes to an ancient Marian Grotto below, near the parish church Our Lady of Victories, which has been a place of worship for centuries. The fresco of the Virgin Mary above the altar is said to have been painted by St Luke. The spring water in the Grotto is credited with medicinal powers.

Malta's largest beach is also one of its most popular

Mosta Rotunda

St Mary's, the parish church of Mosta, was built using money raised by the local community and a voluntary workforce between 1833 and 1860.

The immense parish church, the Mosta Rotunda, in this busy town in the centre of Malta is what attracts visitors. The Rotunda, built in the mid-19th century, has massive walls up to 6m deep. These allowed the enormous dome – the fourth largest in Europe – to be constructed without scaffolding. This amazing building feat, which lasted 27 years, was helped by the older church on the same site which was only dismantled when the new church was complete. Some question the aesthetic harmony of the two belfries and the Ionic columns of the façade fronting such a large dome, but this cannot detract from the beautiful interior, with six side chapels, intricate marble floor and almost three-dimensional murals by Giuseppe Cali. The sacristy contains a replica of a 200kg bomb that pierced the dome in 1942 but fortunately failed to explode amidst the congregation. Two other bombs bounced off the dome without exploding.

INFORMATION

✚ C2
✉ 8km west of Valletta
☎ 21433826
🕐 Daily, 9–noon, 3–5 (religious services after 5PM)
🍴 Cafés and restaurants (£) near the church
🚌 43–45, 47, 49, 50, 53, 56, 57, 65, 86, 149, 157, 427
♿ Few
🎫 Free
🔄 Naxxar (➤ 50–51)

The enormous dome of this church was erected without scaffolding

Museum of Archaeology

INFORMATION

✚ IBC
✉ Republic Street
☎ 21221623
🕐 Summer, daily 7:45–2;
   winter, Mon–Sat 8:15–5,
   Sun 8:15–4:15
🍴 Cafés and restaurants (£)
   within walking distance
↔ Palace of the Grand
   Masters (➤ 42),
   Bibliotheca (➤ 59)

*Right: 'Fat Goddess'
statue on display at the
museum
Below: statue of a knight
of St John outside
Verdala Castle, Rabat.
The knights dined in the
museum's main hall*

The Museum of Archaeology building was once the Auberge de Provence, built in 1575 and home to the most prestigious group of Knights.

Although it has undergone considerable modification over the centuries, it still has its main hall where the Knights dined on iced dishes (remarkably, the ice came from Sicily). The building now houses an important collection of antiquities, and a visit is recommended as a preliminary to seeing the major prehistoric sites in Malta and Gozo. There are important sculptures from the Tarxien Temples (➤ 47), including the bulbous lower half of a fertility goddess that would have stood over 2m high. From Ħaġar Qim (➤ 33) there is a superb limestone altar and there are a number of Roman antiquities, including a huge anchor that was discovered off the northern coast in the 1960s.

National Museum of Fine Arts

Enter the welcome cool and elegant interior of this building to find a minor treasure house of Western European art.

This notable building dates back to the 16th century when it was the palace of a French Knight. Famous figures inhabiting it over the centuries included Charles d'Orleans, brother of King Louis Philippe of France, who died here. For a time it was the British Admiralty House, but was returned to Maltese ownership in 1964; it became the home of the museum in 1972. The whole style of the building, including the magnificent staircase with two flights of semicircular steps, contributes a sense of serenity and elegance to what is a noted collection of art.

On three floors there are 30 rooms full of remarkable paintings. On the first floor, over a dozen rooms display paintings from the 14th to 17th centuries representing Venetian, Dutch and Italian schools. Plaster models by the local artist Sciortino are also here. Mattia Preti is well represented in rooms 12 and 13 with works such as *The Martyrdom of St Catherine*, while room 14 has paintings by Antoine de Favray and is known as Favray's Room. In room 4 are paintings by Domenico Tintoretto (a relative of the famous Tintoretto), Palma il Giovane and Andrea Vincentino.

Rooms 20 to 23 are dedicated to works by Maltese 17th- to 20th-century artists. The museum also displays a particularly fine array of antique Maltese furniture. A display of relics from the era of the Knights may reopen in the basement of the museum.

INFORMATION

➕ IBC
✉ South Street, Valletta
☎ 21233034
🕐 1 Oct–15 Jun, Mon–Sat 8:15–5, Sun 8:15–4:15; 16 Jun–30 Sep, Mon–Sun 7:45–2
🍴 The Scalini restaurant (£) or the union Cafeteria (£) a few metres down in the Workers' Memorial Building
♿ None
💷 Inexpensive

Knights of St John

Palace of the Grand Masters

Situated in Valletta's Palace Square, the official residence of the Grand Masters until 1798 is now home to Malta's Parliament.

The Palace was originally a great house built for the nephew of Grand Master del Monte in 1569.

It was extended two years later by Gerolamo Cassar, commissioned by the knights, into a two-storey building enclosing two courtyards: Neptune Court, with its central bronze statue of Neptune, and Prince Alfred Court, each entered by a separate doorway in the rather plain façade. In Prince Alfred's Court note the Pinto Clock Tower with its mechanical figures, erected in 1745.

Inside, many of the State apartments are decorated with friezes depicting episodes from the history of the Order. There are portraits of the Grand Masters and of European monarchs, interesting furniture and works of art. In the Small Council Chamber are particularly beautiful 18th-century Gobelin tapestries. In the Hall of St Michael and St George, once the throne room, are paintings, notably a frieze showing the Great Siege by Mateo Perez d'Aleccio, a pupil of Michaelangelo. The Hall of Ambassadors is hung with red damask, paintings and another d'Aleccio frieze. The Yellow State Room, where the Grand Master's pages lived, has paintings by Batoni and Ribera.

Prince Albert's Court leads to the Armoury, a converted stables, which for those with children will be the most interesting part of the visit. Here hundreds of exhibits of armour, weaponry and ordnance date back to the siege of 1565. Looking at the armour you understand why the circular steps leading up to the main building are so shallow: one suit weighed as much as 50kg, making it difficult for a knight in full armour to climb them.

The palace dates from 1569 and was extended in 1571

St John's Co-Cathedral and Museum

Its austere, 16th-century exterior belies the stunning baroque interior, where the magnificence and wealth of the Order burgeons in works of art.

Built in the 16th century to a simple Mannerist design by Gerolamo Cassar, this was, until 1798, the Conventual Church of the Order of the Knights of St John. The wide plain façade with the two bell towers of the Co-Cathedral ('Co-' because there are two cathedrals) seems dull. Once inside though, there is almost too much to take in. It is outstanding on several levels: its historical associations, the proportions of its architecture, its rich decoration and the great diversity of its treasures. On promotion, every Knight was required to make a gift to the Order's church.

The interior, once as austere as its exterior, was redesigned in the baroque style under the supervision of Mattia Preti. A central nave has side chapels each dedicated to a different *langue* of the order. On the barrel-vaulted ceiling a series of oil-on-plaster paintings by Preti show 18 episodes in the life of St John the Baptist. The striking floor is paved with the ornate and highly individual multi-coloured marble tombstones of Knights.

Above the crypt, usually closed to the public, is the marble, lapis lazuli and bronze altar. The huge marble group in the apse by Giuseppe Mazzuoli depicts the baptism of Christ. Across the nave is the Chapel of the Blessed Sacrament. Legend says that its silver gates were painted black to make them appear worthless during the looting by Napoleon. Inside is an icon, the *Madonna of Carafa*, presented to the order in 1617.

The Chapel of Auvergne has three works by Giuseppe d'Arena, while the Chapel of Aragon contains the first piece of work done by Preti for the Knights, *St George and the Dragon*. Painted in 1658 in Naples, it was his sample of work aimed at obtaining the commission for the vault.

INFORMATION

✚ IBC

✉ St John's Square, Valletta

☎ 21220536

🕐 Mon–Fri 9:30–12:30,
   1:30–4:30, Sat 9–2.
   Closed public holidays

🍴 Café Marquee (£) is
   opposite

♿ None

💷 Inexpensive

✋ Sunday High Mass at
   9:15AM in Latin and
   masses in the vernacular
   on church festivities and
   days of commemoration

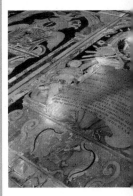

Tombstones of the Knights of St John in the cathedral floor

43

St Paul's and St Agatha's Catacombs

INFORMATION

➕ C3

✉ Triq Sant'Agata, Rabat

☎ 21454562 (St Paul's),
21454503 (St Agatha's)

🕐 Jul–Sep, Mon–Fri 9–5, Sat
9–1; Oct–Jun, Mon–Fri
9–12, 1–5, Sat 9–1. Closed
Sundays and public
holidays

🍴 Cafés and restaurants (£)
near by

🚌 80, 81 from Valletta, 86
from Buġibba, 65 from
Sliema

♿ None

🚻 Inexpensive

*Statue of a robed St Paul
in the catacombs
beneath the Church of
St Paul*

Wander among 3sq km of dimly lit, claustrophobic and eerily empty tombs under the ancient town of Rabat.

St Paul's Catacombs, the largest of Rabat's catacomb complexes, is a labyrinth of corridors and burial chambers. Although plundered many years ago, the empty graves are found in three basic styles. The canopied grave is a little like a four-poster bed, with a flat slab overhung with a canopy cut from the soft limestone rock. Another type is the saddest: the loculus, a tiny rectangular recess cut into the wall to hold the grave of a child. Others called floor graves are cut into the floor and would have been covered with a slab of rock. A thousand corpses must once have rested here. Scattered around the graves are roughly hewn tables with circular benches around them. They were probably used by the families of the recently entombed for a religious service after the burial, or on anniversaries.

Close by, St Agatha's catacombs, below the church, are so named because the saint is said to have lived here for a while to escape the attentions of the Emperor Decius. Fewer catacombs are visited on the 30-minute tour, but there are over 30 frescoes dating back to the 12th to 15th centuries, depicting St Agatha and other Christian figures. Here is the arcosolium type of tomb: arched windows cut into the rock wall. In the convent beside St Agatha's Church is a museum with related and unrelated exhibits, and outside is a good green area where you can rest to recover from the gloom and low ceilings.

St Paul's Cathedral

An ancient cathedral that is a masterpiece in itself as well as a treasure chamber of Maltese baroque art.

The belfries and dome – probably the finest on Malta – dominate the skyline, and the frontal exterior with three balanced bays separated by Corinthian pillars has an altogether grander presence than that of St John's Co-Cathedral in Valletta. This is the finest of Lorenzo Gafà's churches, built between 1697 and 1702. However, the interior, in the form of a Latin cross, may seem gloomy despite the profusion of reds and golds. Numerous frescoes by Preti show events in St Paul's life, including his appearance on a white horse when the city was besieged by Saracens in 1442. The vaulted ceiling is covered in more frescoes by Vincenzo and Antonio Manno. The carved Irish bog-oak sacristy doors were part of the original church which was destroyed in the earthquake of 1693. The floor is covered in the funerary slabs of church and local dignitaries. In the Chapel of the Blessed Sacrament is a 12th-century icon of the Madonna and Child. The marble font is 15th century, while the marquetry stalls date from 1481.

The museum stands on an ancient site, thought to be the villa of Publius, the Roman governor who was converted to Christianity by St Paul. The collection of artwork donated in 1833 includes works by Dürer and Goya, while later donations include *St John the Baptist* by Ferretti and *The Adoration of the Shepherds* by Subleyras. There are vestments of ancient lace, manuscripts and collections of silver and coins. The ground floor has a collection of Punic and Roman items, while the corridor contains the original panels from the 14th-century choir stalls of the cathedral.

INFORMATION

➕ C3
✉ St Paul's Square, Mdina
☎ 21454136 (cathedral); 21454697 (museum)
🕑 Mon–Sat 9–11:45, 1:30–4:30, Sun open only for Mass. Museum Mon–Sat 9–1, 1:30–4:30
🍴 Cafés and restaurants (£–££) near by
🚌 80, 81, 84, 86 from Valletta, 65 from Sliema
♿ None
💷 Inexpensive
🔁 Mdina and Rabat (➤ 37)
❓ Festival of Conversion of St Paul, 25 Jan. Festival of St Peter and St Paul, 29 Jun. Pontifical masses on Church festivals. No admittance to non devotees during church services

Young people prepare for a tour of Mdina

Sliema

INFORMATION

✚ E2

✉ 7km from Valletta

🍴 Plenty of cafés and
restaurants (£–££)

🚌 61–65, 67, 68, 70, 671
from Valletta for ferries,
also 60, 63, 163 from
Valletta, 70 from Buġibba,
65 from Rabat, 86 from
Buġibba and Rabat, 645
from Ċirkewwa, 652 from
Golden Bay

⛴ Valletta–Sliema ferry
(☎ 21335689)

♿ Generally manageable
along Tower Road and
The Strand but the side
streets are often steep
and difficult to manage

🔁 St Julian's, Paceville and
St George's Bay (➤ 51)

Increasingly popular, Sliema is now Malta's most modern tourist centre with excellent transport links, amenities and a superb seafront setting.

Tower Road is its 5-km promenade, full of shops and restaurants, and the road continues north to St Julian's and Paceville. Sliema has no sandy beaches but swimming and bathing off the rocky platforms along Tower Road is popular and there is a lido farther along the road. The southern end of Tower Road joins The Strand, which fronts Sliema Creek. The Strand is packed with bars, restaurants catering for tourists, internet cafés, tour agents, self-catering apartments and hotels.

A short way along The Strand, at a transport point known as The Ferries, there is a bus terminus, a regular 5-minute ferry service to Valletta, Captain Morgan cruises to Comino and elsewhere (➤ 78–79), a hoverboat service to Gozo and, further down the road, the bridge to Manoel Island. At night there are atmospheric views of Valletta across the water from The Strand, always a popular place for Maltese residents to stroll and chat. The side streets into residential Sliema do not lead to any specific sights, but a meandering walk should throw up some of the fine villas built by the Maltese bourgeoisie at the beginning of the 20th century.

The Tigne headland offered the best point for guarding Marsamxett Harbour and Valletta, although the Knights did not build a fort here until 1792. Other forts are dotted along the coastline and one of them is now a popular restaurant on

The Promenade (top) and Tower Rocks (above) at Sliema are increasingly popular

Tower Road. It will not be long before the Tigne headland is transformed by new tourist developments but now it offers a quiet amalgam of British-style pubs and modest tourist accommodation.

Tarxien Temples

The largest of the prehistoric remains was a rich depository of art, created by temple builders, and in striking contrast to the nearby Hypogeum.

The oldest of the three temples in this complex is some 6,000 years old, while the other two were built at later stages, presumably as additions to the original. The South Temple, the first you come to, was the second to have been built. Its central paved square is surrounded by carved stone benches and a ritual fire was probably lit in the centre of this area. There is a stone basin and an altar, both used in the ceremonies that took place. Many remains were found here, including burnt bones of animals, which are represented on the frieze around the next chamber's walls.

The most imposing building, the Central Temple, was the last to be built (c2400 BC), at the peak of the Tarxien period. It too has a central paved area with a hearth for sacrificial fires. One of the side rooms contains a huge bowl carved from a single piece of stone. These rooms were probably secret areas open only to the priesthood. Most of these temples' doorways show bar holes where doors or screens would have been fitted.

The oldest temple, the East Temple, has a similar structure, although it must have been altered to accommodate the middle building. The remains of a small chamber are built into the walls with a tiny hole from which perhaps an oracle spoke. Outside are the stone balls used to roll the huge slabs of stone into place. Behind the temple complex are the ruins of an even earlier building with a possible hypogeum beneath it. To the right of the gate is a stone with cone-shaped indentations: small stone balls found near by suggest a kind of divination device where the movement of the balls predicted the future. Visit the National Museum of Archaeology (➤ 40) to see finds from the site and an impression of how the temples once looked.

INFORMATION

➕ E3
✉ Neolithic Temples Street, Tarxien
☎ 21695578
🕐 1 Oct–15 Jun, Mon–Sat 8:30–4:30, Sun 8:30–3; 16 Jun–30 Sep, Mon–Sun 7:45–1:30
🍴 Nearest place for food in the main square in Paola, a seven-minute walk away (£)
🚌 8, 11, 12, 13, 15, 16, 26, 27, 115, 427
♿ Good
💰 Inexpensive
🔁 Hypogeum (➤ 34)

A reconstructed stone basin on display at the Tarxien Temples

Valletta

INFORMATION

➕ E2 & IBC

Malta's capital city has a visual splendour out of all proportion to its tiny size. It is just one kilometre long and a little over half that width.

Just about all roads and bus routes will take you to Valletta, sooner or later, and your first impression, whether arriving by road or by ferry from Sliema, will be formed by the forbidding fortress-like exterior of the city. The reason is simple: Valletta was built as a fortress by the Knights of Malta to permanently minimise the threat of a Turkish attack. The Knights chose a rocky peninsula in the north of the island as the site for a completely new city that would fulfil this military function while at

Below: horse and carriage 'taxi' stand
Bottom: street in Valletta

the same time provide a civilized home, a city built by gentlemen for gentlemen, as Byron put it. The poet also penned some verse that spoke of Valletta's cursed streets of stairs. You cannot long explore the city without seeing, if not sympathising with his point of view especially if you arrive by ferry and find yourself climbing up the steep streets to access the city's main thoroughfare, Republic Street. But this is to exaggerate; the city is too small to prove exhausting and if the hottest hours of the day are avoided you will be effortlessly enthralled by its buildings and byways.

There is something schizophrenic about Valletta; buzzing with activity during the day and strangely silent at night. This is because not many people actually reside within the city walls and the urban energy of daytime is fuelled mostly by workers who keep to office hours. This dual identity helps make it an attractive city, full of places to visit during the day while at night you can have the tiny metropolis all to yourself.

MALTA & GOZO's
best

49

Towns & Villages

ATTARD

The summer residence of Grand Master Antoine de
Paule, San Anton Palace, is now the official residence of
Malta's president and the gardens are open to the public.
In Attard itself St Mary's Church is a splendid example of
Renaissance church architecture, designed by Tommaso
Dingli when he was only 22 years old.
➕ D3 ✉ 7km southwest of Valletta 🍴 Corinthia Palace Hotel
(££–£££) 🚌 40, 80, 81, 84 ♿ Good 🔁 Balzan & Lija

GHARGHUR

This small village, subdued and picturesque, is hidden
away at the top of a ridge. The town's Church of St
Bartholomew was designed by Tommaso Dingli in 1636
and its gloomy interior does little to detract from
Għargħur's air of antiquity.
➕ D2 St Bartholomew's Church ✉ 7km northwest of Valletta
🕐 Church: Mon–Sat 4–7:30, Sun 6–11:30 and 4–7:30
🍴 Refreshments (£) at the King George VI bar next to the church 🚌 55
♿ None 🔁 Naxxar (➤ below)

*St George's Bay has a
popular beach*

MARSAXLOKK

This is the largest fishing village on Malta, and the
traditional and strong sense of community suggests it will
remain so. Each Sunday morning the quayside becomes
an open-air fish market, and throughout the week good
seafood restaurants serve the local catch.
➕ F2 ✉ 10km southeast of Valletta 🍴 Cafés and restaurants (£–££)
by the seafront 🚌 27 from Valletta, 427 from Valletta and Buġibba, 627
from Paceville ♿ Few 🔁 Marsaskala (➤ 36)

MSIDA

The parish church of St Joseph is worth a visit for its two
altarpieces by Guiseppe Cali. The Ta'Xbiex Seafront,
where yachts berth, offers pleasant views of Floriana
across the water.
➕ E3 ✉ 3km southwest of Valletta 🍴 Cafés and restaurants (£)
within walking distance 🚌 40, 41, 42, 43, 44, 45, 47, 49, 50, 52–54,
56, 57, 60–64, 66–68, 452, 453, 667, 671, 672 ♿ Few 🔁 Valletta
(➤ 48),

NAXXAR

The parish of Naxxar dates back to 1436 and it is said
that after his shipwreck St Paul came here and washed his
clothes out (Naxxar translates as 'to hang clothes to dry').

The quiet suburb of San Pawl tat-Tarġa ('St Paul of the Step'), where St Paul is said to have preached from the steps of the church, is only 1km away. Palazzo Parisio, in the central square, is open to the public, introducing the lifestyle and dwelling place of the rich nobility in 19th-century Malta.

➕ D2 ✉ 9km northwest of Valletta 🍴 Bars and cafés (£) across the road from the church 🚌 54, 55, 56, 65 ♿ Good ↔ Mosta (➤ 39) **Palazzo Parisio** www.palazzoparisio.com ✉ Victory Square, Naxxar ☎ 21412461 🕐 Mon–Fri 10–4 🎫 Inexpensive

The Sunday morning fish market in Marsaxlokk

QORMI

Qormi was once known as Casal Fornaro meaning 'Village of Bakers'. The tall church of St George is a pleasing edifice with a well-proportioned exterior that balances its façade, spires and dome.

➕ D3 ✉ 4km southwest of Valletta 🍴 Nowhere suitable for a meal in the old part of town 🚌 88, 89, 91 ♿ The narrow streets are not wheelchair-friendly ↔ Valletta (➤ 48)

QRENDI

The diminutive Church of St Catherine Tat-Torba is worth a visit if only to wonder at its unique façade. Another oddity, for Malta, is the octagonal Gwarena Tower, while to the south of the village there is a natural wonder known as Il-Maqluba. This huge hole, some 100m across and 50m deep, was presumably caused by the collapse of a subterranean cave.

➕ D4 ✉ 11km southwest of Valletta 🍴 Only a couple of bars (£) 🚌 35, 38, 138 ♿ Good ↔ Ħaġar Qim & Mnajdra (➤ 33), Blue Grotto (➤ 25)

ST JULIAN'S, PACEVILLE AND ST GEORGE'S BAY

St Julian's was a sleepy fishing village that awoke one day in 1798 to find nearly 500 of Napoleon's ships in the bay. Beyond St Julian's , Paceville (pronounced patch-e-ville) is the nightlife capital of Malta. Around the headland of Dragonara Point is attractive St George's Bay, the only local beach area.

➕ E2 ✉ 7km northwest of Valletta 🍴 Plenty of cafés and restaurants (£–£££) 🚌 62–66, 68, 70, 667, 671 from Valletta, 627 between Paceville and Marsaxlokk ♿ Few ↔ Sliema (➤ 46)

A view across to the water to the Maritime Museum at Senglea

SENGLEA

Senglea is one of the historic Three Cities, along with Vittoriosa and Cospicua, where the Knights first settled after 1530. The Safe Haven Gardens, at the promontory's tip, are worth a visit. From the lookout in the gardens there is a truly spectacular view of the Grand Harbour. The stone vedette at the tip carries a sculptured eye and ear, symbols of vigilance.

➕ E3 ✉ 4km (by road) south of Valletta 🍴 Café (£) near the church but consider a picnic 🚌 3 ♿ Good

51

Museums

Mosaic at the Roman Baths in Rabat

LASCARIS WAR ROOMS

The War Rooms were named after a French knight Jean Lascaris who became Grand Master (1636–57). The rooms were dug into the rock beneath Lascaris Bastion, and formed the subterranean headquarters of the island's defence system during the punishing bombardment of World War II. Displays, diagrams, photographs and dioramas complement the carefully refurbished command rooms.

➕ IBC ✉ Upper Barracca Gardens ☎ 21234936 ⏰ Mon–Fri 9:30–4:30, Sat–Sun 9:30–1 🍴 Cafés and restaurants (£–££), walking distance ♿ None 💷 Inexpensive

MALTA AVIATION MUSEUM

Suitably located at Malta's historic World War II airport. The Spitfire and Dakota are two of the prized exhibits. You will also find a good crafts village with stalls in the original RAF Nissen huts.

➕ C3 ✉ Hut 161, Crafts Village, Ta Qali ⏰ Mon–Sat 10–5 ☎ 21416095 💷 Inexpensive

MUSEUM OF ROMAN ANTIQUITIES

Remains of a Roman town house were discovered just outside Mdina in 1881 and the museum is built over the site. Noteworthy exhibits in the main gallery include an olive crusher, discovered at Marsaxlokk, used to extract the pips so oil could be made from the pulp.

➕ C3 ✉ Wesgha Tal-Muzew, Rabat ☎ 21454125 ⏰ 6 Jun–30 Sep, Mon–Sun 7:45–2; 1 Oct–15 Jun, Mon–Sat 8:15–5, Sun 8:15–4:15 ♿ No wheelchair access to the basement 💷 Inexpensive

Outside the National War Museum

NATIONAL WAR MUSEUM

Located under the ramparts facing Marsamxett Harbour, the vaulted hall of the War Museum is packed with hardware, photographs and memorabilia from World War II. One of the most famous exhibits is the wingless Gladiator biplane, *Faith*, the sole survivor of the *Faith*, *Hope* and *Charity* trio of planes that formed Malta's aerial defence in 1940. Also on display is the George Cross that the people of Malta received for their heroism in 1942.

➕ IBC ✉ Lower St Elmo on French Curtain ☎ 21222430 ⏰ 16 Jun–30 Sep, Mon–Sat 7:45–2PM; 1 Oct–15 Jun, Mon–Sat 8:15–5, Sun 8:15–4:15 🍴 Nearest café (£) is at the Sacra Infermeria ♿ Few 💷 Inexpensive (free to senior citizens and students under 19) 🚌 Fort

St Elmo (► 54) 🔉 Lascaris War Rooms (► 52) are of related interest

PALAZZO VILHENA/NATIONAL MUSEUM OF NATURAL HISTORY

The magnificent Palazzo Vilhena, also known as the Magisterial Palace, was built by the Grand Master de Vilhena in the early 18th century. It now houses the National Museum of Natural History.

➕ IBC ✉ St Publius Square, on the right immediately after passing through Mdina Gate ☎ 21455951 (Museum of Natural History) 🕐 16 Jun–30 Sep, Mon–Sun 7:45–2; 1 Oct–15 Jun, Mon–Sat 8:15–5, Sun 8:15–4:15 💷 Inexpensive

ST JOSEPH'S ORATORY

This tiny, interesting museum is on a little square outside the north door of the Church of St Lawrence. Exhibits include the hat and sword worn by Grand Master La Vallette, and curiosities ranging from an early Bible used by the Inquisitors, to a much-used pack of playing cards of 1609.

➕ IBC ✉ Vittoriosa Square 🕐 Mon–Sat 8:30–12, 2–4, Sun 9:30–12 🍴 Café Riche (£) 🚌 1, 2, 4, 6 ♿ Few 💷 Free

TALES OF THE SILENT CITY, MEDIEVAL TIMES AND THE KNIGHTS OF MALTA

These multimedia shows and exhibitions, in palazzos along Villegaignon and Magazine Streets, bring to life the history and lore of Mdina.

Tales of the Silent City ➕ C3 ✉ Palazzo Gatto Murina ☎ 21451932 🕐 Daily 9:30–4:30
Medieval Times ➕ C3 ✉ Palazzo Notabile ☎ 21454625 🕐 Mon–Sat 10:30–4:30
Knights of Malta ➕ C3 ✉ Casa Magazzini ☎ 21451342 🕐 Mon–Sat 10:30–4:30

Faith, *a World War II biplane on display at the National War Museum in Valletta*

Historic Buildings

ARCHITECTURE

Lorenzo Gafa (1639–1710), brother of Melchiorre and famed for his domes, was one of many talented architects whose monuments still stand. Gerolamo Cassar (1520–86) designed a number of Valletta's buildings. including St John's Co-Cathedral, the Grand Master's Palace and all the auberges. His son Vittorio (d1605), with Grand Master Wignacourt, built Forts St Lucian and St Thomas. Others included Nadrea Beli (1705–72), Antonio Ferramolio (d1550) and Francesco Laparelli da Cortona (1521–70).

A guard at Fort St Elmo wearing traditional dress

AUBERGE DE CASTILE ET LÉON

It dates from 1574 but the imposing baroque façade was added in the mid-18th century under Grand Master Pinto, a flamboyant bust of whom decorates the top of the stately doorway. The overall effect is that of baroque architecture at its most graceful and least complicated. The British Army had its headquarters here, and today it houses the prime minister's office.

✚ IBC ✉ Castle Square ⏰ Not open to the public ❚❚ Cafés and restaurants (£–££) within walking distance ♿ Good ↔ Upper Barracca Gardens (➤ 59)

CASA ROCCA PICCOLA

This late 16th-century dwelling was built for the Italian knight Pietro La Rocca and is worth visiting for its period antiques. The bedroom contains a beautiful four-poster bed, the library has an intriguing wall-cabinet that functioned as a portable chapel and the various other rooms have a fascinating variety of antiques and paintings.

✚ IBC ✉ 74 Republic Street ☎ 21231796 ⏰ Mon–Sat 10–4PM. Guided tours on the hour (last tour 4PM) ❚❚ Cafés and restaurants (£–££) within walking distance ♿ Chair-bound visitors can be helped up the stairs and the doors on the first floor are wide enough to accommodate wheelchairs 🎫 Moderate ↔ Palace of the Grand Masters (➤ 42)

FORT ST ANGELO

Records show that a fort called Castrum Maris stood on the site of Fort Angelo in 1274 but it is believed that a building was here long before that, possibly a temple to the Phoenician goddess Asthart. The fort was the British naval headquarters and the base for Allied naval operations in the Mediterranean during World War II.

✚ IBC ✉ Vittoriosa Wharf ⏰ Jun–Sep, Sat 9–1; Oct–May, Sat 10–2. Guided tours every 15 minutes ❚❚ Café Riche (£) 🚌 1, 2, 4, 6 ♿ Some uneven surfaces 🎫 Inexpensive. Ticket covers Fort St Elmo

FORT ST ELMO

The vulnerable tip of the Valletta peninsula was chosen by the Order of St John as the best site for their fortifications. Its star-shaped design allowed for watch towers to be strategically angled so as to guard the entrances to both harbours and the British added gun emplacements in the 19th and 20th centuries.

✚ IBC ✉ End of Republic Street and Merchants Street ⏰ Sat 1–5, Sun 9–5 ❚❚ Café (£) inside the fort ♿ None

🏛 Inexpensive and ticket also covers Fort St Angelo 🔁 National War Museum (➤ 52), Malta Experience (➤ 78) ❓ Alarme! Historical battle re-enactment, 11AM last Sun in month, Feb–Jun, Sep–Oct (☎ 21247523)

INQUISITOR'S PALACE
This building began its life in the Norman period as the Court of Justice but was enlarged and taken over when the Papal Inquisition came to Malta in 1574. The 62 Inquisitors sat here and an unknown number of people were tortured and died at their hands.
➕ IBC ⊠ Main Gate Street ☎ 21827006 🕐 Summer, Mon–Sat 7:45–2; winter, Mon–Sat 8:15–4:30, Sun 8:15–4 🍴 Café Riche (£) 🚌 1, 2, 4, 6 ♿ None 🏛 Inexpensive

PALAZZO FALZON
Built in Siculo-Norman style, notably in the design of the windows and the moulding over the two doorways. The ground floor is a small private museum with naval and harbour paintings. There are displays of antique furniture and 16th- and 17th-century kitchen utensils are displayed in the charming inner courtyard.
➕ C3 ⊠ Triq Villegaignon, Mdina ☎ 21454512 🕐 Mon–Fri 10:30–1, 2:30–4:40 🏛 No entrance fee but a donation is welcomed

PALAZZO SANTA SOPHIA
The date plaque of 1233 makes this the oldest building in Mdina. The ground floor is authentically medieval but the first floor, still true to the Siculo-Norman style, was added in 1938. Look up to the first floor level and you can see the typical horizontal moulded design known as a 'string course'.
➕ C3 ⊠ Triq Villegaignon, Mdina

SACRA INFERMERIA
The Holy Infirmary was one of Valletta's early buildings, receiving its first patients in 1574. It soon became famous for its high standards, as well as its grand interior. The Great Ward, 153m long, has one of the longest unsupported roof expanses in Europe.
➕ IBC ⊠ Mediterranean Street ☎ 21224135 🕐 Mon–Fri 9:30–4:30, Sat–Sun 9:30–4 🍴 Café (£) on the premises 🏛 Inexpensive 🔁 Fort St Elmo (➤ 54) and National War Memorial (➤ 52) ❓ Conducted tours

VERDALA PALACE
This castle-like palace was built in 1586 by a Grand Master as a summer residence It has been renovated and enriched over the centuries but the luxury of its interior cannot be seen by visitors unless it once again opens to the public on certain days of the week.
➕ C3 ⊠ 3km southeast of Rabat 🚌 81 🔁 Buskett Gardens (➤ 59), Clapham Junction (➤ 59), Dingli Cliffs (➤ 59)

Auberge de Castile et Léon, Valletta

The patio of Palazzo Falzon, Mdina

55

Children' Attractions

LOOKING AFTER CHILDREN

Small children are particularly vulnerable to the sun and need to be protected; apply a high-factor sun block regularly, especially after swimming. If you need a child seat in your hire car, make sure to book it in advance and check it carefully on arrival. The same goes for cots and high-chairs in hotels and apartments. Finally, don't forget to check that your balcony railings are secure.

Children, and their parents, will love the flumes at Splash and Fun Park

CLUB NEPTUNE

A waterpolo and swimming club open to non-members on a daily membership basis. The fresh-water pool is heated and there are restaurant and bar facilities. It is located near the Barracuda restaurant on the waterfront.

➕ E2 ✉ Balluta Bay, St Julian's ☎ 21346900 🕐 Daily 8–5 🚌 62, 64, 67, 68, 70 from Valletta, 627 between Paceville and Marsaxlokk

DINOSAURS

Perhaps the best thing about these life-sized reproductions enhanced by animation, sound and lighting, is their location close to the Mdina Glass factory and other craft shops. Children should also enjoy the glass-blowing (▶ 76).

➕ C3 ✉ Ta'Qali National Park ☎ 21416720 🕐 Jun–Sep, Mon–Sat 10–5; Oct–May, daily 11–5:30 🚌 80 from Valletta or Rabat

EDEN SUPER BOWL AND CINEMAS

Consisting of a computerised bowling alley with 20 lanes, a bar and a huge multi-cinema complex (that even spreads to the other side of the road), Eden makes an evening's entertainment for the young. The Paceville location means plenty of fast-food restaurants close by.

➕ E2 ✉ Paceville, St George's Bay ☎ 21319888 🕐 Daily 10AM–12:30AM 🚌 62, 64, 67, 68, 70 from Valletta, 627 between Paceville and Marsaxlokk

HELICOPTER RIDE

One possibility is to combine transport with pleasure and take the children to and from Gozo via helicopter, departing from Malta's international airport and arriving at the Xewkija heliport in Gozo. Sightseeing helicopter flights last either 20 or 40 minutes.

➕ E3 ✉ Malta Air Charter, Luqa ☎ 21662211 (Air Malta), 21557905 (Gozo Heliport), 21243777 (Valletta), 21330646 (Sliema) 🕐 Daily

MDINA DUNGEONS

Pass through Mdina Gate and these medieval dungeon chambers are immediately on one's right: 'Discover Horror, Drama and Mysteries from the dark past'. Young children will love the waxwork scenarios and their gruesome details.

➕ C3 ✉ St Publius Square, Mdina ☎ 21450267 🕐 Daily 9:30–5:30 🚌 80, 83, 86

MEDITERRANEAN MARINE PARK

Dolphins and sea lions, reptiles, swans, wallabies and other creatures are found cavorting here and putting on special shows each day.

➕ D2 ✉ White Rocks, Bahar ic-Caghaq ☎ 21372218 🕐 Apr–Oct, 10:30–1:30, 3:30–5; check in winter 🚌 70 from Sliema or Buġibba, 68 from Valletta

MISTRA VILLAGE

Non-residents may leave their children at an animation show plus disco in the evening, while enjoying a meal in the hotel restaurant, and then join the children later for a show and disco in the amphitheatre.

➕ C2 ✉ Xemxija Hill, St Paul's Bay ☎ 21580481 🚌 43–45, 50, 51, 52

PLAYMOBIL FUNPARK

The German lego-like toy company has a shop, play area and water channels to amuse young children. Tours of the toy factory are sometimes available but telephone ahead.

✉ B36 Bulebel Industrial Estate, Zejtun ☎ 21693763 🕐 Jul–Sep, Mon–Fri 9–6, Sat 6–9PM; Oct–Jun, Mon–Fri 9–5:30 🚌 27–30

SPLASH AND FUN PARK

Next door to the Mediterranean Marine Park, with four water chutes, large pool, restaurant. Adjacent, the Children's Play park is free to enter: model dinosaurs, bouncy castles, bumper cars and the like.

➕ D2 ✉ White Rocks, Bahar ic-Caghaq ☎ 21374283 🕐 Daily 9:30–5 🚌 70 from Sliema or Buġibba, 68 from Valletta

SUN CITY

A leisure centre in Marsaskala comprising four cinemas, a snooker table and a café serving snacks.

➕ F3 ✉ Triq Il-Gardiel, Marsaskala ☎ 21632858 🕐 Daily 10–2, 6:30–11 (later closing summer weekends) 🚌 19, 20, 22

TOYS MUSEUM

There is little in Gozo that is specifically aimed at children but the island still has plenty to offer. The journey there, by boat or helicopter (▶ 56), is pleasantly short and interesting and once on Gozo the Citadel at Victoria has plenty of museums (▶ 31) suitable for children. There is a Toys Museum in Xagħra for younger children. The Gozo 360° audio-visual show on the history and culture of Gozo (▶ 79) is also a possibility.

➕ B4 ✉ Xaghra, Gozo ☎ 21562489 🕐 Apr–May, Thu–Sat 10–1; Jun–Oct, Mon–Sat 10–12, 3–6; Nov–Mar, Mon–Sat 10–1 🚌 64, 65 from Victoria

UNDERWATER SAFARI

Children should enjoy a trip in MV Seabelow's observation keel, for it is below the level of the sea with windows for viewing marine life, including the odd passing octopus. Every passenger has at least 20 minutes in the observation keel during the one-hour trip.

➕ E2 ✉ Captain Morgan Cruises, Dolphin Court, Tigne Seafront, Sliema ☎ 21343373 🕐 Dep from Buġibba from 10AM onwards 🚌 Sliema: 60–64, 67, 68 from Valletta, 70, 86 from Buġibba, 65, 86 from Rabat, 645 from Ċirkewwa, 652 from Golden Bay

DISCOTHEQUES

The usual pattern for Malta's discos is to allow people in for free before about 10PM and until at least 11PM there are few people over 21 on the dance floor. This makes them ideal for teenagers who can safely enjoy the sound and lighting effects and the videos. (▶ 80–81 for details of the more popular discos).

Teenagers will probably want to head for a disco in the evening

Beaches

The Mediterranean has virtually no tide and the beaches are generally safe for children. The water off Malta and Gozo is ideal for diving and snorkelling.

ARMIER BEACH
Situated in the extreme northeast of Malta (bus 50 from Valletta), with few facilities and occasional rough swells but lots of sand.

COMINO'S BEACHES
The Blue Lagoon (➤ 27) is deservedly the most popular spot.

GHAJN TUFFIEHA BAY
Sandy and less crowded than Golden Bay beach yet only a short walk away and reached by steps.

GOLDEN BAY
The most popular beach on the island after Mellieħa Bay because of its extensive stretch of sand.

GNEJNA BAY
Without your own transport there is a 2km walk from Malta's Mġarr, but the worthwhile reward is sand with rocky platforms.

MARSASKALA AND ST THOMAS BAY
There is no sand but coastal bathing is very popular here because of the bay's picturesque location.

MELLIEHA BAY
Malta's most popular beach is 2km north of Mellieħa. Shallow water and lots of sand make it entirely suitable for children.

PETER'S POOL
Not much of a beach but a terrific jumping-off point into crystal-clear, deep water.

RAMLA BAY
The only really sandy beach in Gozo, shallow and safe for swimming.

SLIEMA/ST JULIAN'S
No sand but there are plenty of rocky platforms for sunbathing.

A diving trip in the crystal-clear waters of Paradise Bay

Dwerja Point, Gozo, where the clear water reveals the coral beneath the surface

Free Attractions

In the Top 25

3 **CHURCH OF ST PAUL'S SHIPWRECK (▶ 26)**
16 **MOSTA ROTUNDA (▶ 39)**

BIBLIOTHECA (NATIONAL LIBRARY)

This grand, late 18th-century, Venetian-style building was the last public building commissioned by the Knights. It now houses some 400,000 works, many rare or priceless.

🔳 IBC ✉ Republic Square ☎ 21224338 🕐 16 Jun–30 Sep, Mon–Sat 8:15–1:15PM; 1 Oct–15 Jun, Mon–Fri 8:15–5:45, Sat 8:15–1:15PM 🍴 Cafés (£–££) in Republic Square 🚻 None 🈯 Free 🔁 Palace of the Grand Masters (▶ 42)

BUSKETT GARDENS

These woodland gardens were created under Grand Master Lascaris in the 17th century with the practical purpose of raising hunting falcons. The name is taken from *boschetto* ('little wood') and the gardens reveal a botanically diverse collection of trees, as well as groves of oranges and olives.

🔳 C3 ✉ 4km south of Rabat 🍴 Light refreshments available but a picnic is recommended 🚌 81 🚻 Few 🈯 Free 🔁 Clapham Junction (see below), Dingli Cliffs (▶ below), Verdala Palace (▶ 55)

CLAPHAM JUNCTION

A network of cart ruts, parallel grooves cut into the rock that sometimes cross each other like railway lines. The ruts vary in depth (40–60cm) and width which gives credence to the idea that they were created by wooden sleds made of tree trunks, tipped with iron runners, used to transport goods and materials. during the Bronze Age.

🔳 C3 ✉ 0.5km south of Buskett Gardens 🚌 81 🚻 None 🈯 Free 🔁 Buskett Gardens (see above), Dingli Cliffs (▶ below), Verdala Palace (▶ 55)

DINGLI CLIFFS

The village of Dingli, 253m above sea level, is the highest on Malta and the nearby Dingli Cliffs offer one of the island's most stunning panoramic views. On the edge of the cliff stands the tiny and lonely chapel of St Magdalena that dates back to 1646.

🔳 C3 ✉ 15km southwest of Valletta, 4km south of Rabat 🍴 Bobbyland Bar and Restaurant (▶ 63–64) 🚌 81 🚻 Few 🔁 Verdala Palace (▶ 55)

UPPER BARRACCA GARDENS

These 18th-century gardens on top of St Peter and St Paul's demi-bastion offer excellent views of the Grand Harbour and Vittoriosa across the water. The gardens are dotted with statues, the most interesting being Sciortino's *Les Gavroches*.

🔳 IBC ✉ Castile Place 🍴 Cafés and restaurants (£) within walking distance 🚻 Few 🔁 Auberge de Castile et Léon (▶ 54)

ARCHAEOLOGICAL SITES

Few of Malta's prehistoric sites have been developed for tourism, and the majority stand undisturbed in the middle of farmland. Access is free, but as you are on private land, remember to respect the property of the farmer by leaving everything exactly as you found it.

Cart ruts at Clapham Junction, probably made during the Bronze Age

Places to Have Lunch

Enjoying a meal at one of Valletta's cafés

Seafood and fish are Maltese specialities

L'ANKRA (££)
Walkable from the ferry at Mgarr harbour; good pizzas and some tasty local items like the Gozo cheese ravioli.
✉ 11 Shore Street, Mgarr, Gozo ☎ 21555656 🕐 Daily 11:30–2:30, 6:30–10:30

BLOOMERS (££)
On the main road, this brasserie serves good Mediterranean-style food and salads. Daily specials.
✉ St George's Road, St Julian's ☎ 21333394 🕐 Daily 12–2:30, 6:30–11:30

CAFÉ DAMIER (£)
One of the more elegant places for a spot of lunch along Tower Road, with a few tables on an outdoor balcony.
✉ Sliema Chalet Hotel, 117 Tower Road, Sliema ☎ 21335575 🕐 9AM–10PM

THE CARRIAGE (££)
Brilliant views looking across to Sliema, quality food and crisp white decor combine to make The Carriage a favourite place for an unhurried lunch. Top-notch.
✉ Valletta Buildings, South Street, Valletta ☎ 21247828 🕐 Mon–Fri 12–3, Fri–Sat 7:30–11

CRIANZA (£)
Pasta, pizza (take-away available), pancakes and salads in ancient building with vaulted ceiling.
✉ 33 Archbishop Street, Valletta ☎ 21238120 🕐 Daily 12–3:30, 6:30–11:30

IT-TMUN (££)
Close to the Xlendi seafront, this restaurant is ideal for a slow lunch. The homemade soups are very good.
✉ 3 Mount Carmel Street, Xlendi, Gozo ☎ 21551571 🕐 Wed–Mon 12–3, 6–10:30

PEGASUS (££–£££)
The best value at this air-conditioned, brasserie-style restaurant is the set lunch. Pleasantly informal.
✉ Le Meridien Phoenicia, The Mall, Floriana ☎ 21225241 🕐 Mon–Sat 12–3, 6:30–10:30

PORTO DEL SOL (££)
Splendid views across Xemxija Bay and carefully cooked dishes in a comfortable and formal restaurant.
✉ Xemxija Road, St Paul's Bay ☎ 21573970 🕐 Mon–Sat 12–2:30, 6–11, Sun 12–2:30

THEATRU MANOEL COURTYARD (£)
A delightful little courtyard café. Homemade pies and sandwiches; Maltese specialities; licensed.
✉ Old Theatre Street, Valletta ☎ 21222618 🕐 Mon–Sat 11–3

MALTA & GOZO
where to...

On Malta

PRICES

Approximate prices for a three-course meal for one without drinks and service:

£ = under LM6
££ = LM6–12
£££ = above LM12

STUFFED DELIGHTS

Stuffed dishes are common in Maltese cuisine. Octopus, squid and cuttlefish are all stuffed, as are aubergines, marrows and peppers. Vegetarians should ask for stuffed vegetables without minced meat for this is often added to the onions, tomatoes, herbs and breadcrumbs that make up the filling.

VALLETTA AND FLORIANA

BLUE ROOM (££–£££)

Just by the Palace, this is one of the best Chinese restaurants in Malta. The menu includes a number of set meals and house specials include beef in black pepper and bean curd with minced pork.

✉ 59 Republic Street, Valletta ☎ 21238014 🕐 Tue–Sat 12–3, 7–11

BOLOGNA RESTAURANT (££)

Pasta, meat and fish fill the menu and worth trying are the giant Mediterranean prawns grilled with lemon and parsley. At lunch-time the place can be busy but at night it often takes on a subdued and pleasantly discreet atmosphere.

✉ 59 Republic Street, Valletta ☎ 21246149 🕐 Mon–Sat 12–2:15, 7–10:15

CAFÉ JUBILEE (£)

As with its sister café on Gozo (► 69), this is a popular bistro decked out in 1920 and 30s style. The daily specials are recommended, though there is a menu of standard pasta and salad dishes.

✉ 125 St Lucy Street, Valletta ☎ 21252332 🕐 Daily 8–1AM

CAFÉ MARQUEE (£)

There are tables inside, but only the weather keeps people away from the outdoor tables facing St John's Co-Cathedral. No surprises with the food: pizzas, burgers, pastas, salads, sandwiches and ice-cream.

✉ 9 St John's Square, Valletta ☎ 21236257 🕐 Daily 9–7

CAFÉ PREMIER (£)

Outdoor tables in Republic Square, ideal for people-watching, and a musty interior that looks unchanged from decades ago. Set meals, pizzas, pasta, burgers, lots of drinks and a fairly good vegetarian salad.

✉ Republic Square, Valletta ☎ 21247300 🕐 Daily 8:30–5:30

COCOPAZZO (£)

Cocopazzo is a neat, cultured little restaurant, suitable for lunch or dinner, away from the noise of Republic Street. The Mediterranean food is mostly salads, pasta, chicken and especially fish dishes. Pleasant service.

✉ Valletta Buildings, South Street ☎ 21235706 🕐 Mon–Fri 9–3, 6:30–10, Sat–Sun 12–3, 6:30–10

EDDIE'S CAFÉ REGINA (£)

The interior is brightly lit but the tables outside in Republic Square are even more brightly lit on a warm Mediterranean morning. Pizzas, pastas, grills, milkshakes and one or two Maltese dishes, including qarabaħ (stuffed marrows). Easily distinguished from other cafés in the square by the green coloured tables and waiters' uniforms.

✉ Republic Square, Valletta ☎ 21246454 🕐 Daily 10–10

DE LUCIA (£)

An unpretentious little café, handy for the Museum of Fine Arts in the same street, serving excellent caper and bean salads, light

snacks and good coffee.
Newspapers available.

✉ 28a South Street, Valletta
☎ 21236258 ⏰ Mon–Fri
8–8, Sat 8–1PM. Closed Sun

DA PIPPO (££)

Recommended by a reader,
Da Pippo has also been
discovered by discerning
Maltese to judge by the
stream of locals popping in
for lunch. The menu of
Italian and Maltese dishes
should satisfy most tastes.

✉ 136 Melita Street
☎ 21248029 ⏰ Mon–Sat
11:30–3:30

SCALINI (££)

A small Italian menu with
mostly meat dishes, for
example *scalloppini ai
funghi*. The interior is
pleasantly cool and
unpretentious.

✉ 320 South Street (opposite
the Museum of Fine Arts), Valletta
☎ 21246221 ⏰ Mon–Fri
12–2:30, 7–11, Sat 7–11

BALZAN

CORINTHIA ROOM
RESTAURANT (£££)

The main restaurant of the
Corinthia Palace Hotel and
one of the best in Malta.
The setting is superb. There
is one central dining area
with the surrounding rooms
of the villa forming dining
adjuncts. The whole place is
elegantly furnished and
decorated in a grand style.
European menu.

✉ Corinthia Palace Hotel, De
Paule Avenue, Attard
☎ 21440301 ⏰ Daily
7PM–10PM 🍴 40

IL-MELITA (£)

There are two entrances to
San Anton Gardens (► 50)

and the Il-Melita bar and
pizzeria is situated next to
the one on Birkirkara
Street. Not a touristy
restaurant but a good place
for a drink and meal after
visiting the Gardens.

✉ Birkirkara Street, San Anton
Gardens, Balzan ☎ 21441074
⏰ Mon–Sun 12–2:30, 5–11
🍴 40

BUĠIBBA

GRANNY'S (£)

Recommended by a reader
for its value-for-money
breakfasts, Granny's serves
equally satisfying lunches
and dinners and the price of
drinks is another reason to
call in. Just off Buġibba's
main square.

✉ Pioneer Road ☎ 21378460
⏰ Mon–Sun 9AM–11PM

OUTWEST AGENTINIAN
STEAKHOUSE (££)

Wild West theme for a
restaurant dedicated to
meat: steaks and kebabs are
the favourites but chicken
and burgers are also on the
menu. A small pre-dinner
drinks area.

✉ Empire Cinema Complex,
Pioneer Road ☎ 2158066
⏰ Daily 6–11:30

DINGLI CLIFFS

BOBBYLAND BAR AND
RESTAURANT (£)

At weekends in the summer
the tables are
oversubscribed and there
can be an air of frenzy
about the place. Come at a
quieter time and the view
out to sea will overwhelm.
The food is usually
excellent, with an emphasis
on traditional meat dishes
featuring rabbit and lamb,

FRESH BREAD

If you are up at around six in
the morning you may hear the
loud honking of the bread
delivery van announcing its
arrival in a street. The Maltese
take their bread *(hobza)*
seriously and in villages there
are often two deliveries a day.
Be sure to buy your loaf
before 11AM in the morning.

63

On Malta

A FISH DICTIONARY

MALTESE	ENGLISH
acciola	amberjack
cerna	grouper
dorado	swordfish
dott	stone bass
klamer	squid
pagru	sea bream
san pietro	john dory
pesce sicca	cuttlefish

but the fish is always a welcome alternative.

✉ Panoramic Road, Dingli Cliffs ☎ 21452895 ⏰ Tue–Fri 11:30–2:30, 7–10:30, Sat 11:30–2, 7–10:30, Sun 11:30–2:15, 7–10 🚌 81

MARSASKALA

AL KAFE (£)

A pleasant pizzeria and cafeteria with a prime location on the waterfront and tables filling the pavement under giant umbrellas. There is a pub, Summer Nights, a few doors down under the same management and there is also a guest house.

✉ Marina Street, Marsaskala ☎ 21632528 ⏰ Wed–Mon 8AM–11PM 🚌 19, 22

THE CRAFTY COCKNEY (£)

Situated on the quiet side of the bay, this is a sociable pub and food joint serving familiar dishes like steak and kidney pie, chicken curry and ploughman's.

✉ Triq Is-Salini ☎ 21634070 ⏰ Mon–Sun 10–2:30, 5–midnight 🚌 19, 20

ESCOFFIER (££)

Classier-looking inside than the exterior suggests, the menu has a mixture of Italian, French and Mediterranean dishes. The food is a cut above the average; to find the place walk out of Marsaskala on the Valletta road and take the first left just past the terminal bus stop.

✉ Triq il-Buttar ☎ 21634429 ⏰ Mon–Sat 7–11, Sun 12–3PM

GRABIEL (££)

Probably the most popular restaurant with local people and deservedly so because the prices are reasonable and the food is very good. There is a wide range of starters and while the main dishes are mostly meat the counter is usually overflowing with examples of the locally caught fresh fish. The restaurant is right in the centre of town. Recommended.

✉ Mifsud Bonnici Square ☎ 21684194 ⏰ Mon–Sat noon–2, 5–midnight. Closed 14–28 Aug 🚌 19, 22

JAKARTA (££)

A small but smart interior with white linen tablecloths and a menu of oriental dishes. There is a set meal for two people besides the à la carte choices which include satay, spare-ribs and crispy duck with pancakes.

✉ Triq il-Gardiel ☎ 21639452 ⏰ Tue–Sun 7–11, Sun noon–2PM 🚌 19

TAL-FAMILJA (££)

Past the Sun City cinema, this is a large restaurant with outdoor tables available. The fish and local dishes are likely to be the best items on the menu and vegetarians catered for.

✉ Triq il-Gardiel ☎ 21632161 ⏰ Tue–Sun 12–5, 6:30–2AM

MARSAXLOKK

IR-RIZZU (££)

This is an excellent fish restaurant and it is easily found on the seafront in Marsaxlokk. Meat dishes are available but locals wax lyrical about the variety of fish available and the unerring skill with which it is prepared for the table.

This is partly because the traditional Maltese method of steaming fish is used.

✉ Xatt is-Sjjieda
☎ 21871569 ◉ Daily 12–3, 6:30–10:30 🚍 27 from Valletta, 427 from Buġibba, 627 from Paceville

IS-SAJJIED BAR & RESTAURANT (££)

Comforting views of the sea, which is where the best dishes on the restaurant's menu are caught. There are other Italian-style dishes available but it's the local fish that make Is-Sajjied a rather special place.

✉ Xatt Is-Sajjieda
☎ 21652549 ◉ Mon–Sun 12–2:30, 7–10:30 (closed for dinner on Sun; closed for lunch on Sat) 🚍 19, 22

MDINA AND RABAT

BACCHUS (££)

The bare stone walls of this restaurant once housed Mdina's gunpowder store but, despite a dungeon-like atmosphere, this is one of the best places for a meal in Mdina. There are tasty hors d'oeuvres, speciality fish dishes, grills and pasta; the Grand Opera dessert will have you singing.

✉ Inguanez Street, Mdina
☎ 21454981 ◉ Daily 9–9
🚍 80, 81 from Valletta, 65 from Sliema

CIAPPETTI TEA ROOMS (££)

Lovely courtyard setting with wooden tables and a simple short menu of salads, rolls and home-made cakes. There is an open-air terrace upstairs on the bastion.

✉ 5 St Agatha's Esplanade, Mdina ☎ 21459987 ◉ Daily 11–3:30, 7:30–11 🚍 80, 81 from Valletta, 65 from Sliema

CUCKOO'S NEST TAVERN (£)

This is one of the tiniest restaurants in Malta with three tables and a diminutive bar, but it has character. Nearly all dishes on the menu are meat, featuring beef and lamb.

✉ 9 St Paul Street, Rabat
☎ 21455946 ◉ Daily 11:30–2:30, 7–10 🚍 80, 81, 83, 84 from Valletta, 65 from Sliema, 86 from Buġibba

DE MONDION (£££)

Enjoy a cocktail downstairs in the hotel's grand sitting room before heading upstairs to the open-air terrace where a table is best reserved in advance to ensure a panoramic view of the landscape, dominated by Mosta's dome. Fine Mediterranean cuisine and starters like avocado pear in coriander and tarragon batter served with Aragula and an olive tapenade.

✉ Xara Palace Hotel, Misrah il-Kunsill, Mdina ☎ 21450560
◉ 7:30–10:30 🚍 80, 84 from Valletta, 65 from Sliema

FONTANELLA TEA GARDEN (£)

Panoramic view from the tables of the battlements of Mdina. Only light meals like sandwiches and salads but an excellent selection of homemade cakes – lemon meringue, black forest gateau. Recommended.

✉ 1 Bastion Street, Mdina
☎ 21454264 ◉ Summer, daily 10–10; winter, 10–6 🚍 80, 81 from Valletta, 65 from Sliema

PASTIZZI

The traditional Maltese snack is sometimes translated as cheesecake but this can be misleading. They are in fact made from a rich flaky pastry and a savoury filling of ricotta cheese or dried peas. They are eaten mid-morning or mid-afternoon with tea and coffee. High in calories but friendly to the taste buds.

65

On Malta

FENEK BIZ–ZALZA

Rabbit has been eaten in Malta for as long as anyone can remember and in rabbit stew (*fenek biz-zalza*) the taste has been perfected. The rabbit is fried in a mixture of red wine and fat and then stewed slowly with vegetables, herbs and more wine. Sometimes the rabbit is roasted or served inside a pie along with vegetables and pieces of pork – *torta tal-fenek*.

THE MEDINA (£££)

Located inside an old Norman dwelling, with a vine-laden courtyard for summer meals and a comfortable interior with a fire burning in winter. The food is French, with Italian and Maltese influences here and there. Can be romantic.
✉ 7 Holy Cross Street, Mdina ☎ 21454004 🕔 Mon–Sat 7:30pm–10:30 (closed on public holidays) 🚌 80, 81, 83, 84 from Valletta, 65 from Sliema, 86 from Buġibba

POINT DE VUE (£–££)

There are outdoor and inside tables and some of the Maltese dishes make a refreshing change. (The French and German menus carry more Maltese meals than the English one – a management decision no doubt based on experience). Try the *haruf imsajjar fl-imbio* (spicy marinated lamb in wine) which appears on all the menus.
✉ 5 The Saqqajja, Rabat ☎ 21454117 🕔 Daily 9–11:30 🚌 80, 81, 83, 84 from Valletta, 65 from Sliema, 86 from Buġibba

SB GROTTO TAVERN (£–££)

Step down into this terrific little tavern serving some real surprises. Fondue and *moules mariniere* and an above-average wine list.
✉ Parish Square, Rabat ☎ 21455138 🕔 Daily 12–2:15, 7–10

MELLIEĦA

ALANTIL BAY RESTAURANT (£)

This family-run bar and restaurant serves snacks, grills, salads and burgers. No surprises with the food except for a couple of Maltese dishes like rabbit and *bragioli* (rolled sliced beef filled with ham), but it is inexpensive and reliable and there are outside tables.
✉ 61 G Borg Oliver Street, Mellieħa ☎ 21573049 🕔 Daily 10–1PM 🚌 43, 44, 45 from Valletta, 48 from Buġibba and Ċirkewwa, 645 from Sliema and Ċirkewwa

THE ARCHES (£££)

Centrally located on the main street, The Arches restaurant has long been considered one of the best in Malta. It has a good wine list and the European cuisine is complemented by mouth-watering desserts.
✉ 113 Borg Oliver Street ☎ 21523460 🕔 Mon–Sat 7–10:30 🚌 43, 44, 45 from Valletta, 48 from Buġibba and Ċirkewwa, 645 from Sliema and Ċirkewwa

GIUSEPPI'S WINE BAR (££–£££)

The menu changes according to the season so expect something fresh with the occasional surprise; the daily specials are good value and fresh fish is nearly always available.
✉ 25 St Helen Street, Mellieha ☎ 21574882 🕔 Tue–Sun 7:30–11 🚌 43, 44, 45 from Valletta, 48 from Buġibba and Ċirkewwa, 645 from Sliema and Ċirkewwa

HALF WAY INN (£–££)

As the name suggests, halfway down a hill between the village and the beach. Recommended by a reader for its generous portions, fresh fish and

Maltese dishes. Popular with locals and visitors.

✉ Marfa Road, Mellieħa Bay ☎ 21521637 🕐 Daily 6–12 🚌 43–45 from Valletta, 48 from Buġibba and Ċirkewwa, 645 from Sliema and Ċirkewwa

IL-MULINO (££-£££)

Authentic Italian food at this pretty restaurant. The downstairs indoor section is pleasant while upstairs there is a terrace. Recommended.

✉ 45 Main Street, Mellieħa ☎ 21574045 🕐 Summer, Tue–Sun 7–11; Winter, Tue–Sat 6:30–10:30, Sun 11:30–3PM 🚌 43, 44, 45 from Valletta, 48 from Buġibba and Ċirkewwa, 645 from Sliema and Ċirkewwa

MĠARR

IL-BARRI (£-££)

One of the few places to eat in this area. There are inexpensive pizzas as well as substantial dishes. The bar keeps longer and later hours.

✉ Next to the church in the town square, Jubilee Esplanade ☎ 21573235 🕐 Restaurant: Tue–Sat 12–2:30, 7–10. Bar: 9–3:30, 5:15–midnight 🚌 47

ST JULIAN'S, PACEVILLE AND ST GEORGE'S BAY

THE AVENUE (££)

There is no mistaking the popularity of The Avenue, a gem of a place in an area not noted for quality cuisine. Big portions of good value, tasty food.

✉ Gort Street, Paceville ☎ 21311753 🕐 Mon–Sun 12–2:30, 6–11:30 (closed for lunch on Sunday) 🚌 62, 64–66, 68, 70, 627, 645, 652, 662, 667, 671

BARRACUDA (££)

The original beams of an 18th-century residence still support this waterfront restaurant. The food is Italian but the speciality is always the fresh fish, cooked whole.

✉ 194 Main Street, St Julian's ☎ 21331817 🕐 7–10.30. Closed Sun in the winter 🚌 62, 64, 67, 68, 70 from Valletta, 627 between Paceville and Marsaxlokk

LE BISTRO (££)

Situated at lobby level in the hotel, Le Bistro is worth keeping in mind as one of the very few 24-hour food and drink places of any quality on the island. For fine dining go down the marble staircase to Le Petillant (£££).

✉ Radisson SAS Hotel, St George's Bay ☎ 21374894 🕐 24hrs 🚌 62, 64, 65, 67, 68, 70

CAFFE RAFFAEL (£)

Pizza, pasta, salads and kebabs in a lovely stone-built restaurant. Reserve an outdoor waterfront table. Deservedly busy.

✉ St George's Road, St Julian's ☎ 21332000 🕐 Daily 10–11 🚌 62, 64, 65, 67, 68, 70

COMPASS ROSE (£££)

Fine dining indoors or outside under the stars. Starters like smoked salmon and cavroux cheese and main courses like monkfish and cuttlefish with a potato tart cooked in the ink of the fish. Quality service.

✉ Westin Dragonara Resort, St Julian's ☎ 21381000 🕐 Mon–Sat 12:30–2:30, daily 7:30–11 🚌 62, 64, 65, 67, 68, 70

SWEET DESSERTS

The British influence may account for the puddings but Italy must be thanked for the gelaterias (ice-cream parlours) and Sicily is regarded as the source of kannoli, a dessert that is worth seeking out. It comprises cornets of deep-fried pastry filled with ricotta cheese and sweetened with chocolate.

On Malta

A MALTESE PICNIC

Glorious weather invites a picnic so prepare *hobz biz–zejt* (bread with oil) or purchase it at a coffee shop. Traditionally the farmer's packed lunch, thick bread is dipped in olive oil then spread with pulped tomato before being heaped with olives, capers, garlic, vinegar and salt and pepper.

LA DOLCE VITA (££–£££)

Holds its own as one of the best fish restaurants. Reserve a terrace table to enjoy the view across Spinola Bay.

✉ 159 St George's Road ☎ 21337806 ◷ Daily 12–2:30, 7–11. Closed for lunch in winter 🚍 62, 64, 67, 68, 70 from Valletta, 627 from Marsaxlokk

EASTERN BREEZE (£££)

Asian fusion as its best, this is a contender for the best restaurant in Malta. Everything works, from the service to the food to the neat, Jacobsen-like cutlery, and the sizzling hot chocolate desert caps it all.

✉ Intercontinental Hotel, St George's Bay, St Julian's ☎ 21377600 ◷ Tue–Sat 7–11 🚍 62, 64, 65, 67, 68, 70

LA MALTIJA (££)

The best for Maltese food, with suitably rustic décor. Menu includes *aljotta* and *bragioli*.

✉ 1 Church Street, Paceville ☎ 21339602 ◷ Mon–Sat 6–11 🚍 62, 64, 65, 67

MISFITS (££)

The authentic Maltese dishes on the menu, like rabbit stewed in garlic and wine, make a foray into the teenage jungle of Paceville worth while.

✉ Paceville Avenue, St Julian's ☎ 21331766 ◷ 6:30PM–11:30 🚍 62, 64–66, 68, 70, 627, 645, 652, 662, 667, 671

PEPPINO'S (££–£££)

At lunchtime only the wine bar area is open for pasta and salads, but during the evening the top two floors have tables overlooking the bay and reservations are essential at weekends.

✉ 31 St George's Road, St Julian's ☎ 21373200 ◷ Mon–Sat 12–2:30, 7–11 🚍 62, 64, 65, 67, 68, 70

PICCOLO PADRE PIZERIA (£)

Situated below the Barracuda restaurant in the same old building; as well as pizzas (try the pizzotto) there are pasta dishes and pleasant starters.

✉ 194 Main Street, St Julian's ☎ 21344875 ◷ Daily 6:30–11:30

ST PAUL'S BAY

GILLIERU RESTAURANT (££–£££)

A well-established and renowned restaurant with a seafront location; reserve one of the outside tables. There is a 15 per cent discount for hotel residents.

✉ 66 Church Street, St Paul's Bay ☎ 21573480 ◷ Daily 12:15–2:30, 7:30–11 (bar open 10AM–midnight) 🚍 43, 44, 45, 49, 50 from Valletta, 48 from Cirkewwa

SLIEMA

THE BIG BLUE (££–£££)

Friendly service and an appealing menu of meat, pasta and fish dishes. Reserve an outdoor table to watch the sky turning a deeper shade of blue as night approaches.

✉ Crowne Plaza Hotel, Tigne Street, Sliema ☎ 213491 1536 ◷ Mon–Sun noon–midnight

On Gozo

GOZO

CAFÉ JUBILEE (£–££)

French bistro style, all dark wood and walls plastered with prints and bric-à-brac. The café is conveniently close to Victoria's main square and serves pastries, flans, salads, baguettes.

✉ 8 Independence Square, Victoria ☎ 21558921 ⏰ Mon–Sun 8–1AM

CHURCHILL (£–££)

Overlooking the sea and with tables by the water's edge, a lunch here could easily turn into a lazy afternoon. There is a separate evening menu and a bar that stays open until the last person leaves.

✉ Marina Street, Xlendi ☎ 21555614 ⏰ Mon–Sun 10–late

IL-KARTELL (£–££)

A lively waterside restaurant with a good reputation for fresh fish. There is a helpful explanation on a notice board of the various types of local fish. A speciality is mixed seafood with cream, but assorted pizzas are also available. Musical entertainment at night.

✉ Main Street, Marsalforn ☎ 21556918 ⏰ Thu–Tue 11:30–3:30, 7–10:30 (Closed weekdays Nov–Jan) 🚌 21 from Victoria

IL-TMUN (££–£££)

Near the centre of town in a quiet street, with tables on the pavement as well as inside. The food is Mediterranean plus some really good authentic Maltese dishes; the best place for fine food in Xlendi.

✉ 3 Mt Carmel Street, Xlendi ☎ 21581787 ⏰ Wed–Mon 12–3, 6:30–10 (Closed Tue–Thu in Jan, most of Dec and Feb)

L-IMGARR HOTEL RESTAURANT (£££)

Perched on a hill above the harbour, with tables on the terrace, the Sicilian chef in this restaurant serves up wonderful food. The flambé dishes are a speciality and the fish is cooked to perfection.

✉ L-Imgarr Hotel, Triq St Antnin, Mgarr ☎ 21560455/7

JEFFREY'S (££)

A modest and friendly restaurant, with a small open-air section at the back. The food is delicious, and while the menu follows what is locally available at the time, visitors may depend on fish, rabbit and pasta.

✉ 10 Triq I–Gharb ☎ 21561006 ⏰ Mon–Sat 7–10 🚌 2, 91 from Victoria

OLEANDER (££)

A cosy little family-run restaurant, surrounded by oleanders, serving delicious Maltese favourites.

✉ 10 Victory Square ☎ 21557230 ⏰ Tue–Sun 11:30–3, 6:30–10

TRATTORIA (££)

For a more formal dining experience there is the L'Ortolan downstairs, but the Trattoria is pleasingly informal with a diverse menu that caters for vegetarians, and fresh herbs from the hotel's gardens.

✉ Kempinski Hotel, San Lawrenz ☎ 22115620

DELICIOUS AND DIFFERENT

Look for *bigilla*, a dish served with toasted bread that originated during the privations of World War II when there was little choice of food. Mashed beans are mixed with a pumpkin sauce to make this delicious repast. Cumin and garlic give it a spicy taste. Served at the Barracuda in St Julian's (➤ 67).

A CHEESE WITH ATTITUDE

Imported cheeses from Italy are readily available but it would be a pity to miss out on *gbejna*. This cheese made from goat's milk is now made in Malta but it is best enjoyed in Gozo from where it originates. The peppered version (*tal-bzar*) is far tastier than the unpeppered.

On Malta

PRICES

Expect to pay for a double
room per night in summer:
£   = under LM20
££   = LM20–40
£££ = over LM40

VALLETTA

BRITISH HOTEL (£–££)
The longest established
hotel in Valletta has a lovely
situation overlooking the
Grand Harbour. All 44
rooms on six floors have en
suite facilities and
telephone, and some have
balconies. There is a rooftop
sundeck for sun bathing
and drinks and an
inexpensive restaurant.
www.britishhotel.com
✉ 40 Battery Street, Valletta
☎ 21239022

**GRAND HARBOUR
HOTEL (£)**
A superb location with
outstanding views of the
Grand Harbour and an
inexpensive restaurant. The
rooms can be small and
facilities are basic but
nevertheless this still
represents value for money.
www.grandharbourhotel.com
✉ 47 Battery Street, Valletta
☎ 21246003

HOTEL OSBORNE (££)
Recommended by a reader,
the Osborne is a smart
place to have a room if
staying in Valletta. It has an
air of elegance, a pleasant
dining room, a bar and a
lounge area.
www.osbornehotel.com
✉ 50 South Street, Valletta
☎ 21232127

BALZAN

**CORINTHIA PALACE
HOTEL (£££)**
One of the top hotels in
Malta. The rooms have
everything from fax points
to hairdryers and the hotel's
health spa is state-of-the-
art with sauna, massage,
gym, mudstream baths,
aroma-therapy and
reflexology. Indoor and
outdoor pools and tennis
and squash courts complete
the fitness facilities.
www.corinthiahotels.com
✉ De Paule Av, Balzan
☎ 21440301 🚌 40

MELLIEĦA

**LUNA HOLIDAY
COMPLEX (££)**
Self-catering apartments in
a modern complex with a
pool, sun terrace, bar,
restaurant, fitness room and
mini-market. A bus stop is
near by and its only a short
walk to the beach. Studios,
sleeping up to three, plus
one- and two-bedroomed
apartments are available;
May to October and
minimum three-day stay.
www.searchmalta.com/luna
✉ Marfa Road, Mellieħa Bay
☎ 21521645 🚌 44, 45 from
Valletta, 48 from Buġibba and
Ċirkewwa, 645 from Sliema and
Ċirkewwa

**MELLIEĦA HOLIDAY
CENTRE (££)**
This Danish-run complex
comprises 150 self-catering
bungalows, each with two
bedrooms, Olympic-sized
swimming pool, restaurant,
bar, playground and super-
market. The bungalow tariff
is reasonable and in winter
enters the budget category.
✉ Mellieħa Bay
☎ 21573900; dff@vol.net.mt
🚌 43

RABAT

POINT DE VUE (£)
This family-run budget
guesthouse is in a 17th-
century building and

apparently guests have been
staying here since 1898.
The location is central, just
outside Mdina Gate.
www.mol.net.mt/point/
 5 Saqqaja Square, Rabat
☎ 21454117
🚌 80, 81, 83, 84, 86, 65

ST JULIAN'S, PACEVILLE AND ST GEORGE'S BAY

CORINTHIA SAN GORG (£££)
The St George's Bay area is
being developed as an
accommodation centre and
the San Gorg holds pride of
place. All 250 rooms on the
six floors have a balcony
and sea view. The water
facilities are first class and
there are health and fitness
facilities.
www.corinthoahotels.com
✉ St George's Bay, St Julian's
☎ 21374114
🚌 62, 64, 65, 67, 68, 70

HOTEL SAN GORG (£)
Rooms have en suite
showers, 24-hour reception
desk, bar, restaurant and the
hotel is located in the heart
of Paceville. This is not a
quiet retreat, but if you
want to be close to pubs
and discos the Hotel San
Gorg is good value for
money.
www.sangorghotel.com/
✉ Ball Street, Paceville, St
Julian's ☎ 21376685
🚌 62, 64, 65, 67, 68, 70

ST GEORGE'S PARK COMPLEX
With over 800 beds, there
is quite a range of rooms,
studios and apartments on
offer here. The hotel's lido
has two pools and there is a
good leisure centre with

squash courts, sauna and
gym. Certainly not
everyone's cup of tea and
definitely not a place for
quiet relaxation.
www.sgp.com.mt
✉ Dragonara Road, St
Julian's ☎ 21351146 🚌 62,
64, 65, 67, 68, 70

LA VALLETTE RESORT (£££)
An all-round resort that
welcomes families and with
a host of facilities – pools
for adults and children and
a heated indoor one for
winter, gym, squash courts
– as well as five bars and a
restaurant.
www.sgp.com.mt
✉ Dragonara Road, St Julian's
☎ 21351146

VILLA ROSA (££)
This brightly coloured hotel
seems quite homely
compared to the new giant
hotel blocks that are
gradually dominating the
area. The Villa Rosa offers
indoor and outdoor pools,
sports, gym and restaurant
and easy access to nearby
restaurants and Paceville's
dynamic nightlife.
✉ St George's Bay, St Julian's
☎ 21342707 🚌 62, 64, 65,
67, 68, 70

ST PAUL'S BAY, BUĠIBBA AND QAWRA

THE COASTLINE (£££)
Panoramic views of Salina
Bay. There is a shuttle bus
to and from Buġibba, but
this might not be ideal for
guests who want lots of late
nights where the action is.
There is no excuse for not
keeping fit here: an
excellent gym, sauna,

ON THE MOVE
Budget-conscious visitors to
Malta and Gozo who plan to
travel around the islands
staying in different hotels and
guest houses each night
should collect from the tourist
office a useful little brochure
that lists all one- and two-star
hotels, hostels and guest
houses and explains the
available facilites.

On Malta

STAYING PUT

Visitors whose stay in Malta does not exceed three months are classified as non-residents. Anyone wishing to stay longer is required to show proof that their income will enable them to live independently in Malta. Temporary residents become subject to local taxes after six months.

indoor pool and tennis courts are on the premises.
www.islandhotels.com
✉ Coast Road, Salina Bay
☎ 21573781 🚌 70, 449, 645, 652 stop outside

CORINTHIA MISTRA VILLAGE CLUBHOUSE (£££)

This self-catering 'tourist village' is ideal for families. Well-organised, well-equipped apartments and a host of facilities and activities; tennis court, squash courts, fitness centre, sauna and pools. Children's pools, a play area, theatre and organised activities.
www.corinthiahotels.com
✉ Xemxija Hill, St Paul's Bay
☎ 21580481 🚌 43, 44, 45, 50

PRIMERA (££)

Showing its age a little, but still a comfortable abode in the heart of Buġibba, close to the sea and promenade. Most of the eighty-plus rooms have small balconies. A heated indoor pool, rooftop terrace, child-friendly.
www.primerahotel.com
✉ Pioneer Road, Buġibba
☎ 21573880 🚌 43, 44, 45, 49, 50 from Valletta, 48 from Ċirkewwa

SEA VIEW HOTEL (£)

A small pool at the front of the hotel, suitable for children, and adjoining bar. Karaoke sessions twice a week, live music on Friday nights, pool table and internet service. Full- and half-board available; open all year.
✉ Qawra Road
☎ 21573105; fax: 581788

SOL SUNCREST HOTEL (£££)

With over 400 rooms, the Sol Suncrest manages to avoid being impersonal and it has the best facilities of any hotel in the area. There are five restaurants, to suit all tastes and pockets, a disco, two lidos and two outdoor pools, tennis and squash courts, a health centre and a water sports centre. Facilities for people with disabilites are very good.
www.suncresthotel.com
✉ Qawra Coast Road, Qawra
☎ 21577101 🚌 48, 49, 51, 70, 86

SLIEMA

PARK HOTEL (££–£££)

A chic six-storey hotel with modern art and fake marble giving a swank look to the lobby. Restaurant, café, indoor pool, sauna and fitness room. Child-friendly. Half-board available.
www.parkhotel.com.mt
✉ Graham Street
☎ 21343780 🚌 60, 61, 62, 63, 64, 67, 68 from Valletta

PLAZA & PLAZA REGENCY HOTEL (££)

In a prime location on the seafront, this hotel has a pool and restaurant. All the rooms have air-conditioning, and the more expensive benefit from a sea view.
✉ 251 Tower Road
☎ 21341295;
plaza@aghl.com.mt
🚌 60, 61, 62, 63, 64, 67, 68 from Valletta, 70, 86 from Buġibba, 65, 86 from Rabat, 645 from Ċirkewwa, 652 from Golden Bay

On Gozo

GOZO

KEMPINSKI SAN LAWRENZ RESORT & SPA (£££)

Hard to beat the hideaway location of this five-star hotel; it seems to be camouflaged. Inside, all is splendid luxury and the restaurants are some of the best on the island. Plus pools, squash and tennis courts.
www.kempinski-gozo.com
✉ Triq il-Rokon, San Lawrenz
☎ 22110000

L-MGARR HOTEL (£££)

It is worth trying to reserve one the rooms overlooking the harbour for the superb views at this small hotel with a surprising array of facilities: pools, gym, sauna, boat rentals, good restaurant and shuttle bus to Victoria.
✉ Triq St Antnin, Mgarr
☎ 21560455/7

SAN ANTONIO (£–££)

A family-run guesthouse with air-conditioning, swimming pool, separate children's splash pool, and a restaurant. Each if the 13 rooms has its own terrace or balcony. Sea views from the main terrace. Good feedback from previous visitors.
www.clubgozo.com.mt
✉ Tower Street, Xlendi
☎ 21563555 🚌 87 from Victoria

LANTERN GUESTHOUSE (£)

A family-run B & B in the centre of town, with a small restaurant. A friendly establishment with a good reputation.
✉ Qbajjar Road, Marsalforn
☎ 21556285
🚌 42, 43 from Victoria

MARSALFORN GUESTHOUSE (£)

Located close to the seafront, its 20 rooms offer economical accommodation. There is a small restaurant. Basic, clean and well-managed.
✉ Rabat Road, Marsalforn
☎ 21556147 🚌 21 from Victoria

ST PATRICK'S HOTEL (£££)

One of the best hotels in Gozo, it is situated right on Xlendi Bay close to the local restaurants, shops and bars. Most rooms have balconies with views of either the sea, the country-side or a courtyard. Rooftop spa and sun deck.
www.vjborg.com/stpatricks
✉ Xlendi ☎ 21562951
🚌 87 from Victoria

TA'CENC HOTEL (£££)

A strong contender for the best hotel in Malta and Gozo. It is in a tremendous location, overlooking cliffs and sea with views across to Malta and Comino. All 83 rooms are stylishly decorated and have a terrace or small private garden. Facilities inclued tennis courts, swimming pools and a there is a private rocky beach with its own restaurant/bar. Accommodation includes family rooms, suites and stone-built *trulli* bungalows with beehive roofs.
www.vjborg.com/tacenc
✉ Sannat, Gozo ☎ 21556819
🚌 52 from Victoria

BUYING A PROPERTY

Non-Maltese visitors can buy and sell most types of property, over a minimum value of LM15,000, after obtaining a permit from the Ministry of Finance (☎ 21236306). Only one property can be owned at any one time and the funds used to buy must be transferred from abroad. Property agents are easy to find, especially in the Sliema area, and *The Times* on Mondays and Thursdays has especially large rental listings.

Markets

WHEN AND WHERE

Shops in Malta and Gozo generally open Monday to Friday at 9AM and often close for a couple of hours in the afternoon before re-opening around 4PM and finally closing at 7PM. On Saturday shops are usually only open for the morning, but on Sunday very few open. The largest concentrations of shops are in Valletta, Sliema and Rabat.

VALLETTA

OPEN AIR MARKETS

There are two open air markets in Valletta. Triq il-Merkanti (Merchants Street) is mostly clothes and accessories, religious icons, CDs and videos. On Sunday a very busy market opens up in St James' Ditch, near the Triton Fountain, and although it does get frenzied at times there is also a more interesting collection of bric-à-brac, which might appeal to visitors, who will also enjoy watching the activity.

✉ Triq il-Merkanti (Merchants Street) and St James' Ditch, Valletta ◷ Triq il-Merkanti: Mon–Sat 7–noon; St James' Ditch: Sun 6:30–1PM

INDOOR MARKET

Valletta's indoor market is mostly devoted to food and this is the place to visit the day before you leave Malta to make a last-minute purchase of *ġbejna* (Gozitan cheese). It may not be available in sealed packets but it will keep fresh for the flight home and once put in the refrigerator the shelf life of this cheese is at least one month. The peppered version (*tal-bzar*) is highly recommended for those who prefer a stronger cheese.

✉ Triq il-Merkanti (Merchants Street) where the open air market ends ◷ Mon–Sat 6:30–PM

AROUND MALTA

MARSAXLOKK OPEN AIR MARKET

Basically a fish market, but worth a visit even for those who are not actually making a purchase. The variety of shapes and colours of the Mediterranean fish here is surprising, making an attractive scene; and what you see here may well end up on your own plate when you visit one of Marsaxlokk's excellent fish restaurants.

✉ Along the water front, Marsaxlokk ◷ Sun 7–11:30AM 🚌 from Valletta, 427 from Buġibba, 627 from Paceville

OTHER OPEN AIR MARKETS

Many towns in Malta have an open air market once or twice a week and they are worth visiting if you are in the area, but do not go out of your way to make a special trip. They are not tourist markets, but they do provide a welcome opportunity to mix with Maltese people going about the daily business of shopping and meeting friends.

✉ Birkirkara, near the Church of St Helen ◷ Wed, Fri 7–11AM 🚌 41, 42, 71, 78

✉ Birżebbuġa, in St Catherine Street near the Government Primary School ◷ Thu 7–11AM 🚌 11, 115

✉ Naxxar, 21st September Ave ◷ Thu 7–11AM 🚌 54, 55, 56, 65

✉ Rabat, opposite St Paul's Parish Church ◷ Sat 7–11AM 🚌 80, 81, 83, 84, 86, 65

✉ Vittoriosa, St Margherita Heights ◷ Tue 7–11AM 🚌 1, 2, 4, 6

Handicrafts, Arts & Antiques

VALLETTA

ARTISANS CENTRE
One of the best shops for a general selection of quality handicrafts. The jewellery section has handsome Maltese crosses on chains. Picture frames, prints, souvenirs and gifts are also available.
✉ 9 and 10 Freedom Square and 288 Republic Street, Valletta ☎ 21246216 ◷ Mon–Fri 9–1, 4–7, Sat 9–1

GALEA PAINTINGS
The studio and gallery of the artist Aldo Galea. The subject is Malta, especially shipping scenes. The work sells for between LM15 and LM150. Posting and packing service.
✉ 8 Merchants Street, Valletta ☎ 21243591 ◷ Mon–Fri 9:30–1, 4–7, Sat 9:15–12:45

GIO. BATTA DELIA
Fine chinaware and glass from around the world – Wedgwood, Waterford, Spode, Belleek, Minton, Dresden, Cristal Lalique – and an export service. There is also a small branch in Sliema at 76 Tigne Street (☎ 21332924).
✉ Ferreria Palace, 307 Republic Street, Valletta ☎ 21233618

VINCENZO ATTARD
One little workbench, in the corner of this small shop, turns out chains, earrings, plain and filigree, and adjustments can be made to suit the customer. Also check out the Silversmith's Shop, at number 218.
✉ 77 Republic Street, Valletta ☎ 21246192 ◷ Mon–Fri 10–7, Sat–Sun 10–3

AROUND MALTA

EMPIRE ARTS AND CRAFTS CENTRE
This huge crafts emporium sells just about everything. The lace work, paintings, glass and ceramics take second place to the largest selection of jewellery in Malta.
✉ 20A/B St Agatha Street, Rabat ☎ 21453245 ◷ Mon–Sat 10–6 🚌 80, 81, 83, 84, 86

GALLERIA CREMONA
Marco Cremona is a Maltese artist who studied in Italy and London and worked as an art teacher before turning professional. His paintings have been exhibited in Europe and his work, usually impressions of Malta, sells for between LM75 and LM500; prints are a lot less expensive.
✉ 16 Museum Road, Rabat ☎ 21450509 ◷ Summer: Mon–Sat 10–6. 🚌 80, 81, 83, 84, 86

GREENHAND LEATHERCRAFT
This little shop, bound to be passed on a walk through Mdina, has two branches. The action in the workshop can be seen and, as well as leather goods, lace and gifts are on sale.
✉ 2 Magazine Street and 28 Villegaigon Street, Mdina ☎ 21454689 ◷ Mon–Sat 10–6

LIN'S LACE
This shop can be relied upon throughout the year for jewellery, crafts, local wine, pottery and garments.
✉ Triq Bieb, Mdina ☎ 21563022 ◷ Mon–Sat 9:30–5

WHAT TO BUY

Maltese handicrafts are the best items to take home. Apart from the glass, choose from filigree silver jewellery, Maltese crosses, gold jewellery, lace work and ceramics. Italian clothes tend to predominate in the boutiques in Sliema.

75

Handicrafts, Arts & Antiques

LACE

Gozo is renowned for its hand-made lace, a traditional home-based activity that began life as a devotional act by pious women making lace adornments for their local church. Shawls and tablecloths are the most popular items and prices are reasonable. Rabat in Malta and the Citadel in Gozo are the best places to make a purchase.

MDINA GLASS

Decorative glass is made in the traditional manner by hand and mouth; also etching and crystal cutting.

✉ Ta' Qali Craft Village, Ta' Qali ☎ 21415786 ◉ Jun–Oct, Mon–Fri 8–6, Sat 8–12:30, Sun 9–4 (Mar–Oct); Nov–Jun, Mon–Fri 8–4, Sat 8–12:30 🚌 80 from Valletta or Rabat, 86 from Buġibba , 65 from Sliema

PHOENICIAN GLASSBLOWERS

Even if no purchase is made, it is still interesting to watch the process of glass being mouth-blown and hand made. The beautiful blues and yellows of the glass are many visitors' favourites.

✉ Ta' Qali Crafts Village, Hut 140 ☎ 21437041 ◉ Mon–Sat 9–4:30

TA'QALI CRAFT VILLAGE

The site is a disused airfield from World War II and the crews' Nissen huts are now devoted to the peaceful business of retailing lace, glass and other crafts. Mdina Glass have their workshop here.

✉ Ta'Qali ☎ 21415786 ◉ Mon–Fri 8–4:30, Sat 8–12:30

TRES CHIC ANTIQUE GALLERY

Antiques from the Mediterranean, as well as Britain and Ireland.

✉ Main Street, Mosta ☎ 21417305 ◉ Mon–Sat 9:30–noon, 4:30–7 🚌 43, 44, 45, 49, 53, 56, 57

WELCOME TO THE LACE SHOP

This small shop situated near St Paul's is packed with lace tablecloths and matching napkins. Most of the items are hand-made but there is also some less expensive machine-made lace.

✉ 5 Triq San Kataldu, Rabat ☎ 21454290 ◉ Mon–Fri 9:30–5, Sat 9:30–3:30 🚌 80, 81, 83, 84, 86

GOZO

BASTION LACE

More than one little shop sells handicrafts in the Citadel, but only attractive hand-made lace is sold in this delightfully tiny shop. Friendly service, no undue pressure to buy.

✉ Bieb l-Imdina Street, Citadel, Gozo ☎ 21561471 ◉ Mon–Sat 9:30–5

LAI THAI

Come to Gozo and leave with handicrafts from Thailand or India! Lots of items small enough to fit into your luggage and an adjoining snack bar to pause and consider before making your final decision.

✉ G. Borg Street, Victoria ☎ 21553313 ◉ Mon–Sat 9–4:30

TA'DBIEGI CRAFT VILLAGE

There is nothing craft-like about the premises: characterless low-level British military huts converted into shops. Pottery, art, lace and clothes account for most of the merchandise.

✉ On the main road between Ta' Pinu Church and San Lawrenz ☎ 21556202 ◉ Daily 8:30–6:45 🚌 2, 91 from Victoria

Souvenirs & Shopping Centres

VALLETTA

GOPALDAS ORIENTAL BAZAAR

Two floors of gifts from Malta and the Orient. There is little of real quality but for inexpensive souvenirs and gifts the place is worth a quick browse.

✉ 33 Republic Street, Valletta
☎ 21224938 ◷ Mon–Sat 9:30–7, Sun (Apr–Oct) 10–1

AROUND MALTA

J M JEWELLERS

A reasonable range of affordable jewellery in this well-positioned shop on the promenade. There is another jewellers a few doors down, so prices can be compared.

✉ 30 Islets Promenade, Buġibba
☎ 21583863 ◷ Jun–Sep, Mon–Sun 9–10; closing earlier during the winter.

MDINA SOUVENIRS

Old coins, glass, prints and lace, including a good selection of hand-made brass door knockers. This little shop also hires out multilingual audio guides with a map to facilitate one's walkabout in Mdina.

✉ 1 St Publius Square, Mdina
☎ 21415436 ◷ Mon–Sat 9–5 (occasional Sun in Jul, Aug)
🚌 80

STOCKHOUSE

There are souvenirs galore plus gifts in this popular, inexpensive tourist shop. There are also knitted woollen garments for sale for those who can overcome the psychological barrier of contemplating them when the island's temperatures are ferocious.

✉ Islets Promenade, Buġibba
☎ 21571554 ◷ Mon–Sat 9–10, Sun 9–1 🚌 49 from Valletta, 48 from Ċirkewwa, 51 from Għajn Tuffieħa, 70, 645, 652, from Sliema, 86 between Buġibba and Rabat, 427 between Buġibba and Marsaxlokk

GOZO

ARKADIA SHOPPING CENTRE

This is the largest shopping centre on Gozo and here you will find a department store, boutiques, shoewear shops and a fast-food outlet. There is a smaller shopping centre in the complex that is home to the Gozo tourist office (► 88).

✉ Fortunato Mizzi (end of Republic Street) ☎ 21558333 ◷ Mon–Sat 9–7

GOZO GLASS

The glass-making workshop is on show inside the shop. Some people find Gozo glass gaudy and flashy, but there are beautiful examples to be found here, and a visit is recommended. The shop is on the main road just outside Gharb on the road to Victoria.

✉ Triq Il-Gharb, Gozo
☎ 21561974 ◷ Mon–Sat 9–6 (Workshop closes at 3:30, Sun 10–4) 🚌 2, 91

JOE XUEREB

Hand-carved and hand-decorated sculptures using Gozo stone. The best pieces look as if they might be thousands of years old, and not cheap.

✉ Ta' Peppi, Bahhara Street, Għajnsielem, Gozo
☎ 21553559 ◷ Daily 10–4

GLASS

One of the best buys is glass and there are three main types. The blue and green Mdina glass is probably the most widely distributed in shops and it can be seen being made at Ta'Qali (► left). Phoenician glass, a characteristic deep blue, is made on Manoel Island (► left) and is also available in good shops. Vibrantly coloured Gozo glass, the most expensive, is best purchased on Gozo (► left).

Trips & Shows, Casinos & Cruises

A DAY TRIP TO SICILY?

Day trips to Sicily, using a catamaran to make the crossing in 1.5 hours, depart early in the morning and arrive back in Malta late at night. The trip usually includes various excursions by coach to places like Mount Etna. Some visitors have found it an exhausting day and an expensive one.

VALLETTA

THE MALTA EXPERIENCE

If time and inclination restrict you to visiting just one of the multilingual audio-visual, large-screen presentations about Malta and Gozo then this is the one to see. The theatre is set inside the historic 16th-century Sacra Infermeria (▶ 55) and the show sets itself the daunting task of presenting Malta's history from Neolithic times onwards in 50 minutes. With the help of 3, 000 colour slides and 39 projectors it does this well. Access for visitors with disabilities, restaurant and souvenir shop.

www.themaltaexperience.com
✉ St Elmo Bastion, Mediterranean Street, Valletta
☎ 21243776 🕐 Mon–Fri on the hour 11–4, Sat-Sun 11–1PM

ST JAMES CAVALIER CENTRE FOR CREATIVITY

Films, theatre, music recitals and art exhibitions take place on a regular basis during the day and there are occasional evening events. There is a shop and a coffee bar, not open at weekends.
✉ Ordnance Street
☎ 21223200; info@sjcav.org
🕐 Mon–Sun 10–5

THE WARTIME EXPERIENCE

A film covering Malta during the years of World War II and made up of archive film recording what happened the and suffering endured by the Maltese people.
✉ Embassy Complex, St Lucia's Street, Valletta ☎ 21227436
🕐 Daily 10–1; on the hour, every hour

AROUND MALTA

CASINOS

The Dragonara Casino, Malta's original casino, has a bar and restaurant and a dress code that stipulates a jacket and tie (these can be borrowed if necessary). The Oracle casino is more geared to tourists, has a number of bars and restaurants, and the dress code is smart/casual, no shorts to be worn after 8PM.
www.dragonara.com
✉ Dragonara Casino, St Julian's
☎ 21382362 🕐 8:30–4AM
🚌 62, 64, 67, 68, 70 from Valletta, 627 between Paceville and Marsaxlokk; free transport from Sliema and St Julian's
www.oraclecasino.com
✉ Oracle Casino, Qawra Seafront, St Paul's Bay
☎ 21570057 🕐 Sun–Thu 10AM–4PM, Fri–Sat 10AM–6AM

CLUB DE BINGO

Bingo halls do not come any posher than this one situated opposite the Dolmen hotel in Qawra.
✉ Dolmen Street, Qawra Seafront, Qawra ☎ 21577677; info@clubdebingo.com 🕐 Daily 10–11

CRUISES

Captain Morgan is a well-established tour company offering a variety of cruises on a regular basis. Harbour cruises depart from Sliema daily, from 10:30AM, and there is also a daily day-long cruise around Malta and Comino, a Blue Lagoon cruise, sunset cruise, overnight cruise, a Party Boat that departs Sliema at 8:30PM and an underwater safari (► 57). Harbour cruises and other trips are also run by Luzzo Cruises from Marsaskala.

www.captainmorgan.com.mt

✉ Captain Morgan Cruises, Dolphin Court, Tigne Seafront, Sliema ☎ 21343373 🚌 60, 61, 62, 63, 64, 67, 68 from Valletta, 70 from Buġibba, 65 from Rabat, 86 from Buġibba and Rabat, 645 from Ċirkewwa, 652 from Golden Bay 🚢 Valletta-Sliema ferry (☎ 21335689)

✉ Luzzo Cruises, 29 Marina Promenade, Marsaskala ☎ 21332669

HELICOPTER RIDE

Combine transport with pleasure and visit Gozo via helicopter, depart-ing from Malta's international airport and arriving at the Xewkija heliport in Gozo. Sightseeing helicopter flights lasting either 20 or 40 minutes are also available.

✉ Malta Air Charter, Luqa ☎ 21662211 (Air Malta), 21557905 (Gozo Heliport), 21243777 (Valletta), 21330646 (Sliema) 🕐 Daily

THE MDINA EXPERIENCE

An audio-visual, multilingual spectacular spanning some 3,000 years of Mdina's history. This is presented in a suitably ancient building. The 30-minute show runs continuously every half hour. Coffe shop.

✉ 7 Mesquita Square, Mdina ☎ 21454322 🕐 Mon–Fri 10:30–4, Sat 10:30–2 🚌 80, 83, 86 from Valletta, 65 from Sliema

GOZO

BOAT TRIPS

Pleasure trips lasting half a day or a full day depart from Mgarr harbour. The trips take in Gozo, Comino and the Blue Lagoon. Fishing trips and watersports are also available. There are meeting points for free transport at Xlendi and Marsalforn.

✉ Xlendi Pleasure Cruises ☎ 21555667 (Marsalforn), 21562548 (Xlendi) 🕐 Dep 11, return 5:30 🚌 21 from Victoria for Marsalforn; 87 for Xlendi

GOZO 360°

Not to be outdone by similar shows in Malta, Gozo now has its very own sound-and-vision show, lasting half an hour, designed to bring the smaller island's own culture and history to life.

www.xlendicruises.com

✉ Castle Hill, Rabat, Gozo ☎ 215559967 🕐 Mon–Sat, every hour between 10:30 and 4:30, Sun every hour between 10:30 and 1:30 🚌 from Mgarr

SUNSET CRUISE

The boat leaves Mgarr in July and August in the evening and the first port of call is Comino. Gozo cheese and *hobz biz-zejt* (bread with oil, pulped tomato, olives and seasonings) are one way to keep hunger pangs at bay as the boat proceeds to Popeye Village in Malta, and then to Comino where it anchors for dinner.

✉ Frankie's Gozo Diving Centre ☎ 21551315 🕐 Dep 5PM, return 11PM 🚌 25 from Victoria

HOLLYWOOD OF THE MEDITERRANEAN

Malta has become the location for a number of Hollywood blockbusters, including *Gladiator* (2000), starring Russell Crowe, and *Troy* (2004), starring Brad Pitt, as well as BBC dramas like *Daniel Deronda* and *Byron*. Full details of the various locations can be accessed via www.visitmalta.com.

Bars & Discos

BARS AND PUBS

The British influence means that pubs are not uncommon in Malta or Gozo and there is tremendous variety in the kind of entertainment they offer. The smallest village is likely to have a tiny bar where visitors are welcome but the only diversion will be a conversation with fellow customers. Valletta's nightlife is non-existent, so for bright lights and live music head for Paceville (pronounced PATCH-eh-vill) or Buġibba.

BARS

MALTA

B.J.S

This pub has a soul. Small stage for bands, often very good, and usually a pleasant upbeat atmosphere despite the dark and smoky interior. Jazz evenings featured. Recommended.
✉ Ball Street, Paceville, St Julian's ☎ 21337642 ◷ Daily, 7–late 🚍 64, 67, 68, 70 from Valletta, 627 between Paceville and Marsaxlokk

BAR NATIVE

This pub does not encourage the under-25s and the music is not so loud that you cannot hear yourself speak. Wine by the glass or bottle and six types of draught beer. Sofas, bar stools and oudoor tables.
✉ St George's Road, Snata Rita Steps, Paceville ☎ 21380635 ◷ Daily 11–late (winter: 6:30–late)

LEMON AND LIME

Tables spill onto the pavement in this popular Marsaskala watering hole which always seems to be the last place to close. Cocktails and snacks available. For quieter drinking, try the Crafty Cockney directly across the water.
✉ Marina Street, Marsaskala ☎ 21829950 ◷ 9AM–late

MISFITS

Not to be confused with the restaurant of the same name (► 68), this is as close to being a laid-back joint as you can muster in heady Paceville. The crowd is mostly Maltese, vaguely alternative, and the atmosphere is relaxing.
✉ Paceville Avenue, St Julian's ☎ 21331766 ◷ late 🚍 62, 64– 66, 68, 70, 627, 645, 652, 662, 667, 671

THE PUB

Also known as Ollie's Last Stand, this was the pub where actor Oliver Reed collapsed and died during the filming of *Gladiator*. Photos of the star adorn the walls of this tiny pub.
✉ 136 Archbishop Street, Valletta ☎ 21237525 ◷ Daily 10-4

SADDLES PUB

This pub has been around for a long time and, as one of the photographs on the wall makes clear, was once very popular with the British army. Still lively with a good atmosphere.
✉ G Borg Oliver Street, St Julian's ☎ 21339993 ◷ Daily, 9–3AM 🚍 62, 64, 67, 68, 70 from Valletta, 627 between Paceville & Marsaxlokk

GOZO

IL-KARTELL

One of the more popular little bars in Marsalforn and a lively enough place as the night wears on. There is a billiards table and, although there is only taped music, sitting on the balcony and sipping drinks in this picturesque fishing village is a pleasant way to spend an evening.
✉ Marsalforn waterfront ☎ 21556918 ◷ 8:30PM–1AM 🚍 21 from Victoria

THE ROOK

Set in an old fort by the sea,

The Rook is one of Gozo's better nightclubs.

✉ Qbajjar, Marsalforn
☎ 21563769 ◷ Mon—Sun 7—Late

BUĠIBBA-QAWRA

While the Paceville area is popular with hip young Maltese, the Buġibba-Qawra area attracts mostly tourists. Hotels like the Suncrest and the Coastline (▶ 72) provide floor shows. There is also dancing and live music from country and western to karaoke.

✉ Coastline, Salina Bay, Salina
☎ 21573781

HERITAGE

Food and drink in this very British and very popular pub and diner in a street across the road from the Primera. There is a cheap pizzeria next door but you won't beat Heritage when it comes to the price of a pint. Check out their website.
www.heritagepub.com

✉ Gandofli Street, Buġibba
☎ 21585677 ◷ 9—late

DISCOS

MALTA

AXIS

Apart from the main dance floor, there is also the Freestyle club that plays less frantic music and, up on the floor above, a small designer-style bar with a tiny dance space and Salsa music setting the mood. Open every night through the summer, Axis has been around a long time and has regained its popularity.

✉ Triq San Gorg, St Julian's
☎ 21373830 ◷ 9:30—4AM

🚌 62, 64, 67, 68, 70 from Valletta, 627 between Paceville & Marsaxlokk

THE BLACK ROSE

The New Dolmen Hotel hosts one of the most popular late-night dancing scenes.

✉ New Dolmen Hotel, Qawra
☎ 21581510 ◷ Daily 8—late, summer only 🚌 48, 49, 51, 70

FRENCHIES

Hotel discos are not always the wildest affairs and Frenchies is fairly sedate compared to Paceville to around midnight, but it attracts a good crowd of people. Wednesday is Ladies' night, Friday is Singles' night and men pay at the door after midnight.

✉ Crown Plaza Hotel, Tigne Street, Sliema ☎ 21341173
◷ Wed—Sat 10:30PM—late
✉ 🚌 60—64, 67, 68 from Valletta, 70, 86 from Buġibba, 86 from Rabat

REEDS

This popular open-air disco in Marsaskala is on the road to St Thomas Bay.

✉ Triq Il-Gardiel, Marsaskala
☎ 21684482 ◷ Fri—Sun 8—late 🚌 19, 20, 22

GOZO

LA GROTTA

Not the most advanced sound system, but this open-air disco is delightful. An amazing location, with the bar in a cave, and a separate pub two minutes away. Opens at 11PM but doesn't come alive until early the next morning.

✉ Xlendi Road, Xlendi, Gozo
☎ 21551149 ◷ 11PM—6:30AM 🚌 87 from Victoria

BUĠIBBA BARS

The place to be for young folk in Buġibba is where Pioneer Road meets the promenade. A cluster of popular bars and numerous eating places near by makes this a natural meeting place and drinkers from pubs like the Bonkers, Coconut Creek and the Victoria spill outside and loudly share the pavement.

Sports

HEALTH CLUBS

A number of the better hotels have health and leisure clubs and some of them can boast excellent facilities. The best of all is the Athenaeum at the Corinthia Palace (► 70) but the following are also very good: Livingwell Fitness Centre at the Hilton Hotel; the World Class Fitness Centre and Thalassoterapie Spa at the Fortina Hotel (☎ 21343380); the Thalgo Marine Centre at the San Lawrenze Hotel in Gozo (☎ 21558640). Some of these operate a temporary membership scheme.

ATHLETICS

THE MALTA AMATEUR ATHLETICS ASSOCIATION

Contact the association to see what events are being organised during your stay. Cross-country and track-and-field events are held fairly regularly.

✉ Room 4, Matthew Micollef, St John Athletic Stadium, Marsa ☎ 21247675 🚍 43, 44, 45, 49, 53, 56, 57

BOWLING

For 10-pin bowling visit the Eden Super Bowl (► 56). There is a shop and a licensed bar.

CYCLING

Gozo is especially appealing by cycle and bikes can be hired from On Two Wheels, Volcano Street, Marsalforn or from Mayjo, Republic Street, Victoria ☎ 21556678. On Malta, try Nova, 153 St George's Road, St Julian's ☎ 21344743 or Agius, Pioneer Corps Road, Buġibba ☎ 21571603.

DIVING

Scuba divers are well catered for and 30- and 40-metre dives get clear visibility. A useful brochure from the tourist board has a map showing the most popular dive sites and other helpful information.

THE ASSOCIATION OF PROFESSIONAL DIVING SCHOOLS

Details of all registered diving companies.
www.dig.gate.net/divers
✉ Msida Court, 61/2 Msida Sea Front, Msida ☎ 21336441

DIVE CLUBS/SCHOOLS

There are many BSAC-, CMAS- or PADI- certified schools on both Malta and Gozo. Along with internationally recognised training courses, they also offer boat or shore dives for both experienced and novice divers alike. Discover the dramatic underwater scenery, drop offs, caves, reefs and the marine life in the clear Mediterranean waters. Equipment for hire. Some of the well-established diving clubs include:
www.divemed.com
✉ Dive Med, Marsascala, Malta ☎ 21639981
www.scubamalta.com
✉ Strand Diving Services, St Paul's Bay, Malta ☎ 21574502
www.digigate.net/meldives
✉ Meldives, Mellieha, Malta ☎ 21522595
www.gozodive.com
✉ St Andrews Divers, Xlendi Bay, Gozo ☎ 21551301
www.atlantisgozo.com
✉ Atlantis Diving Centre, Marsalforn, Gozo ☎ 21554685

GOLF

Golf was introduced to Malta in 1888 and a nine-hole course was established in Floriana. The present 18-hole course at the Marsa Sports Club was re-grassed a few years ago and some 50 sand bunkers added. Temporary membership at the Marsa Sports Club (► below) allows visitors to use the course. A useful brochure from the tourist board describes the nine most interesting holes.

ROYAL MALTA GOLF CLUB

✉ Marsa Sports Club, Aldo Moro St Marsa ☎ 21233851 🚌 1, 2, 3, 4, 5, 6, 8, 11, 12, 13, 15, 18, 19, 21, 26, 29, 32, 34, 35, 36

SPORTS CENTRES

MARSA SPORTS CLUB

Malta's largest sports centre, 4km south of Valletta, has the only 18-hole golf course, cricket ground, mini golf, tennis courts, squash courts, billiards, fitness centre and a bar and restaurant. Join on a daily/weekly basis. ✉ Aldo Moro Street, Marsa ☎ 21233851 🕐 Mon–Fri 9–9, Sat–Sun 9–5 🚌 1, 2, 3, 4, 5, 6, 8, 11, 12, 13, 15, 18, 19, 21, 26, 27, 29, 32, 34, 35, 36

SOCCER

Soccer is very popular. Games (mostly played between September and May) are best watched at the National Stadium.

MALTA FOOTBALL ASSOCIATION

www.mfa.com.mt ✉ 280 St Paul Street, Valletta ☎ 21222697

WATER SPORTS

SAILING AND YACHTING

Between Malta, Gozo and Comino there are nearly 30 anchorages, and places to hire boats include Marsamxett Harbour and Mellieha Bay. Summer

sailing regattas include the Comino regatta in June and the Malta-Syracuse race for keelboats in July. The Royal Malta Yacht Club at Manoel Island (www.rawsilk.com/rmyc ☎ 21333109) has information on chartering yachts. Enquire also at the Vikings Sailing Club Nautical School, Floriana ☎ 21452868, the Cavalieri Hotel Sailing Club, St Julian's ☎ 21336255 or Malta Yatch Charter www.maltayatchcharter .com ☎ 21335771

MALTA SAILING CLUB

✉ 21 Msida Rd, Gzira ☎ 338253 🚌 60, 61, 63, 64, 66, 67, 68, 671

SPORT FISHING

Fishing Mania has a boat insured for up to six people. Leaves Marsaskala or Ta Xbiex at 8:30AM and returns in the afternoon. Depart at 8:30PM for night bottom fishing, returning at 2AM. Includes tackle, bait and snacks. www.mol.net.mt/Fishingmania ✉ Fishing Mania, 20, Flat 4, Old Anchor Court, Buttar Street, Marsaskala ☎ 21632470 🚌 19, 20, 21

WATER SKIING

Water skiing can be arranged through many of the large hotels. Between April and October, Paradise (details below) offer a range of watersports. ✉ Paradise Diving and Watersports, Paradise Bay Hotel, Ċirkewwa ☎ 21574116; paradise@global.net.mt

SNORKELLING AND DIVING

Both snorkellers and divers should fly a code-A flag or tow a surface marker buoy to alert speedboat traffic. Popular snorkelling spots include the west coast just north of Bahar-ic-Caghaq, while a more deserted place is the Ghar Qawqla beach near the Hotel Calypso at Marsalforn, Gozo. Go past the hotel and up the flight of steps near the public toilets.

MALTA & GOZO
practical matters

7 TA' GUNJU 1919

WHAT YOU NEED

		Some countries require a passport to remain valid for a minimum period (usually at least six months) beyond the date of entry — contact their cnsulate or embassy or your travel agent for details.	UK	Germany	USA	Netherlands	Spain
●	Required						
○	Suggested						
▲	Not required						
Passport/National Identity Card			●	●	●	●	●
Visa (regulations can change, check before booking your trip)			▲	▲	▲	▲	▲
Onward or Return Ticket			●	●	●	●	●
Health Inoculations			▲	▲	▲	▲	▲
Health Documentation (Reciprocal Agreement Document, ➤ 90)			▲	▲	▲	▲	▲
Travel Insurance			○	○	○	○	○
Driving Licence (national or international)			●	●	●	●	●
Car Insurance Certificate (if own car, specific to Malta)			●	●	●	●	●
Car Registration Document (if own car)			●	●	●	●	●

WHEN TO GO

Malta

High season

Low season

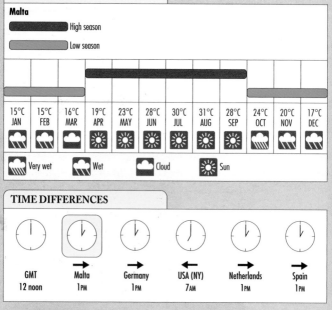

15°C JAN	15°C FEB	16°C MAR	19°C APR	23°C MAY	28°C JUN	30°C JUL	31°C AUG	28°C SEP	24°C OCT	20°C NOV	17°C DEC

Very wet   Wet   Cloud   Sun

TIME DIFFERENCES

GMT 12 noon	Malta 1PM	Germany 1PM	USA (NY) 7AM	Netherlands 1PM	Spain 1PM

TOURIST OFFICES

In the UK (also responsible for Eire)
Malta Tourist Office
Unit C Parkhouse,
4 Northfields, London SW18 1DD
☎ 020 8877 6990
Fax 020 8874 9416
www.visitmalta.com
office.uk@visitmalta.com

In the USA (also responsible for Canada)
Malta National Tourist Office
65 Broadway Suite 823
New York, NY 10006
☎ 212 430 3799
Fax: 425 795 3425
www.visitmalta.com
office.us@visitmalta.com

WHEN YOU ARE THERE

ARRIVING

The national airline, Air Malta (☎ 21 69 08 90), operates scheduled flights from major European cities; there are also charter flights. Gozo has no airport. There are ferry and catamaran services from southern Italy and Sicily to Malta (Valletta). Embarkation cards to be filled in *before* passport control.

Malta (Luqa) Airport to city centre	Journey times	
	🚇	N/A
8 kilometres	🚌	20 minutes
	🚗	15 minutes

Grand Harbour (Valletta) to city centre	Journey times	
	🚇	N/A
1 kilometre	🚌	N/A
	🚗	2 minutes

MONEY

The monetary unit of Malta is the Maltese lira (plural: liri), which is abbreviated to LM.

The lira is divided into 100 cents (c) and there is a further subdivision of cents into mils. Though there are no longer any mil coins you may come across them in prices. Coins are in denominations of 1, 2, 5, 10, 25 and 50 cents and 1 lira, and notes come in 2, 5, 10 and 20 liri.

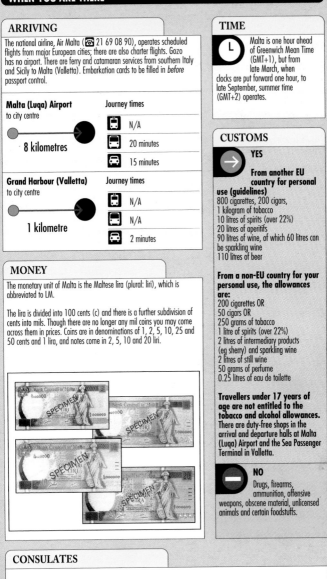

TIME

Malta is one hour ahead of Greenwich Mean Time (GMT+1), but from late March, when clocks are put forward one hour, to late September, summer time (GMT+2) operates.

CUSTOMS

YES

From another EU country for personal use (guidelines)
800 cigarettes, 200 cigars,
1 kilogram of tobacco
10 litres of spirits (over 22%)
20 litres of aperitifs
90 litres of wine, of which 60 litres can be sparkling wine
110 litres of beer

From a non-EU country for your personal use, the allowances are:
200 cigarettes OR
50 cigars OR
250 grams of tobacco
1 litre of spirits (over 22%)
2 litres of intermediary products (eg sherry) and sparkling wine
2 litres of still wine
50 grams of perfume
0.25 litres of eau de toilette

Travellers under 17 years of age are not entitled to the tobacco and alcohol allowances. There are duty-free shops in the arrival and departure halls at Malta (Luqa) Airport and the Sea Passenger Terminal in Valletta.

NO
Drugs, firearms, ammunition, offensive weapons, obscene material, unlicensed animals and certain foodstuffs.

CONSULATES

UK
☎ 233134/5/6
(High Commission)

Germany
☎ 336531 or 336520
(Embassy)

USA
☎ 241240
(Embassy)

Spain
☎ 39 06 6840401
(Resident in Rome)

TOURIST OFFICES

Malta – Head Office
● National Tourism Organisation
  280 Triq ir Repubblika
  (Republic Street)
  Valletta CMR02
  ☎ 21224444/5
  Fax: 220401
  info@visitmalta.com
  www.visitmalta.com

Local Tourist Information Offices

Malta
● 1 City Arcades, Valletta
  ☎ 21237747

● Malta (Luqa) International Airport
  Arrivals Hall
  Gudja
  ☎ 23696073

Gozo
● Tigrija Palazz
  Republic Street
  Victoria (Rabat)
  ☎ 21561419

NATIONAL HOLIDAYS

J	F	M	A	M	J	J	A	S	O	N	D
1	1	2	(1)	1	2		1	2			3

1 Jan	New Year's Day
10 Feb	Feast of St Paul's Shipwreck
19 Mar	Feast of St Joseph
31 Mar	Freedom Day
Mar/Apr	Good Friday
1 May	Workers' Day
7 Jun	Sette Giugno (Commemoration of 7 June 1919)
29 Jun	Feast of St Peter and St Paul
15 Aug	Feast of the Assumption
8 Sep	Victory Day
21 Sep	Independence Day
8 Dec	Feast of the Immaculate Conception
13 Dec	Republic Day
25 Dec	Christmas Day

OPENING HOURS

○ Shops	● Restaurants
● Offices	● Museums
● Banks	○ Cafés

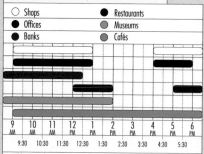

9 AM	10 AM	11 AM	12 PM	1 PM	2 PM	3 PM	4 PM	5 PM	6 PM
9:30	10:30	11:30	12:30	1:30	2:30	3:30	4:30	5:30	

In addition to the times shown many shops in tourist areas stay open throughout the day. In Valletta shops close at 1PM Saturday, and except for a few in Bugibba, shops are closed Sunday. Offices open earlier but do not re-open for the afternoon during the height of summer. Banks open 8:30AM to 12:45PM in winter. Banks also open Friday 2:30 to 4PM (4:30 to 6PM, winter) and Saturday 8 to 11:30AM (8:30 AM to noon, winter). Banks, business, shops and museums are closed on National Holidays. Restaurants and bars remain open.

ELECTRICITY

The native power supply: 220/240 volts.

Type of socket: 3 square-hole type taking square plugs with 3 square pins (as used in the UK). Visitors from continental Europe should bring an adaptor; US visitors bring a voltage transformer.

TIPS/GRATUITIES

Yes ✓   No ✗

Hotels (if service not included)	✓	10%
Restaurants (if service not included)	✓	10%
Cafés/bars	✓	change
Taxis	✗	
Porters	✓	20c a bag
Chambermaids	✓	50c a week
Usherettes	✗	
Hairdressers	✓	10%
Cloakroom attendants	✓	cents
Toilets	✓	cents

PUBLIC TRANSPORT

Helicopter
The fastest and most convenient way to travel between Malta and Gozo is by helicopter (➤ 56)

Cross-Island Buses
Most of Malta's towns and villages are connected to Valletta by bus. Fares are between 7c and 30c. Usually they depart from and return to City Gate (the main terminus). Buses (yellow with an orange stripe) are numbered but their destination is not shown. However, billboards showing the destination and route number can be found in the City Gate Bus Terminus and the tourist office dispenses a free bus map. On Gozo, buses (grey with a red stripe) serve the main villages from Victoria but only run in the morning. Bus passes for 1, 3, 5 and 7 days may be purchased at the Valletta or Buġibba terminals or the sliema ferry terminal
☎ 21250007; www.atp.com.mt

Ferries
Ferries from Malta to Gozo (Mġarr) depart from Ċirkewwa (20-minute crossing) or Sa Maison (75 minutes). Services are frequent. In summer there are also passenger-only hover-marine services from Sa Maison to Mġarr (25 minutes) and from Sliema (30 minutes); some trips via the island of Comino. For information about all services ☎ 21243964/5/6.

Urban Transport
Valletta is the only major conurbation on Malta but as driving is virtually impossible around the city most people walk. From the main bus terminus at City Gate buses are destined for other parts of the island, except for bus 98 which follows a circular route around Valletta, and is probably your best bet.

CAR RENTAL

Hire rates vary but as mileage and insurance is included, it is cheap for Europe. Companies such as Avis (☎ 21225986/7/8), Europcar (☎ 21388516) and Hertz (☎ 21314636) accept credit cards but may ask for a cash deposit. Signposting is poor and so is road quality.

TAXIS

Mostly white Mercedes with distinctive 'taxi' sign on roof. They do not cruise but can be picked up at the airport, hotels, harbours, central ranks or by phone. Black taxis also operate, at cheaper rates, but need to be booked by telephone.
Wembley Motors
☎ 21578025

CONCESSIONS

Students/Youths Holders of an International Student Identity Card (ISIC) can take advantage of concessions for students, including reductions of between 15 and 40 per cent on transport, exhibitions, restaurants and shops, while entrance to museums is free.

Senior Citizens Malta, a popular destination for senior citizens, offers low-cost long-stay winter packages. However, apart from a reduction on some museum fees, there are no specific discounts available.

DRIVING

Speed limits:
There are no motorways on Malta or Gozo

Speed limits on country roads: **40mph (64kph)**

Speed limits in built-up areas: **24mph (40kph)**

Must be worn in front seats at all times and in rear seats where fitted.

Random breath-testing. Never drive under the influence of alcohol.

Petrol (super grade and unleaded) is readily available. Service stations open 7AM–6PM (4PM Saturday); some to 7PM in summer. On Sundays and public holidays a few stations open on a rota basis 8AM–noon, so make sure you have enough fuel in the tank on Saturday night if planning an excursion. Petrol stations do not accept cheques or credit cards.

If involved in a road traffic accident, call the police immediately (☎ 191 in Malta; ☎ 21562044 on Gozo), and *do not* move the vehicle as it may invalidate your insurance. In the event of a breakdown there are three breakdown companies: RMF (☎ 21242222), MTC (☎ 21320349) and CAA (☎ 21696690). If you break down in a hired car, call the hire company to request help.

PHOTOGRAPHY

What to photograph: the natural surroundings provide some dramatic settings – spectacular pastel-coloured cliffs contrasted by rich turquoise seas.
Light: the fierce light of the midday sun should be avoided; clear early morning light or the golden light of sunset are preferable.
Film: most well-known brands of colour print or transparency film are available but you may have difficulty finding fast-speed or black and white film.

PERSONAL SAFETY

You have little to fear in Malta since the crime rate is low and the Maltese are generally honest and courteous. The police (*pulizija*) – blue uniforms similar to British police – have a station in every town and village. Report any crime to them immediately. Some precautions:

● Leave valuables in the hotel or apartment safe, not on the beach.
● Don't make yourself an obvious target for bag-snatchers or pickpockets.
● Don't leave valuables visible in a car.

Police assistance:
☎ **191** (in Gozo: 21562044) from any call box

TELEPHONES

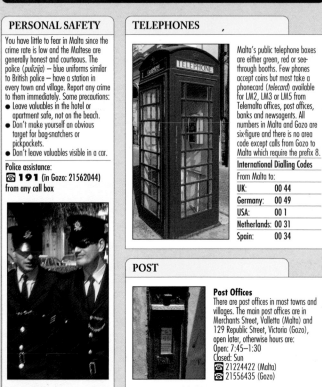

Malta's public telephone boxes are either green, red or see-through booths. Few phones accept coins but most take a phonecard (*telecard*) available for LM2, LM3 or LM5 from Telemalta offices, post offices, banks and newsagents. All numbers in Malta and Gozo are six-figure and there is no area code except calls from Gozo to Malta which require the prefix 8.

International Dialling Codes

From Malta to:	
UK:	00 44
Germany:	00 49
USA:	00 1
Netherlands:	00 31
Spain:	00 34

POST

Post Offices
There are post offices in most towns and villages. The main post offices are in Merchants Street, Valletta (Malta) and 129 Republic Street, Victoria (Gozo), open later, otherwise hours are:
Open: 7:45–1:30
Closed: Sun
☎ 21224422 (Malta)
☎ 21556435 (Gozo)

HEALTH

Insurance
Nationals of UK and certain other countries staying less than 30 days receive free medical treatment within the Maltese health service, but prescribed medicines must be paid for. However private medical insurance is advised for all.

Dental Services
Dental treatment must be paid for. If you need a dentist enquire at the hotel reception desk or call directory enquiries (☎ 190 on Malta; ☎ 890 on Gozo). Private medical insurance covers dental treatment and is advised for all visitors.

Sun Advice
The Maltese islands bask in virtual year-round sunshine; it is almost non-stop April to September. The sun is at its strongest during July and August when wearing a sunhat and covering up the skin is recommended. No topless/nude sunbathing is allowed.

Drugs
On Malta, pharmacies, usually known as chemists, are recognisable by a neon green cross sign. They sell most international drugs and medicines over the counter or by prescription. They open normal shop hours with a Sunday roster.

Safe Water
Tap water is quite safe though not very palatable. Water from fountains should be avoided as it may not come directly from the mains supply. Bottled 'table' water is available everywhere at a reasonable cost along with imported mineral water.

LANGUAGE

Maltese and English are the official languages of Malta and Gozo. Almost everyone speaks English but it is Maltese that is normally heard on the streets and that predominates in the media. Maltese comprises a vast element of words of Italian, French and English origin. The alphabet consists of 29 characters: a, b, ċ (as ch in 'church'), c, d, e, f, ġ (as g in 'George'), g, ħ (as h in 'house'), h, i, j, k, l, m, n, għ (a single letter and usually silent), o, p, q, r, s, t, u, v, w, x, ż (as z in 'zebra') and z. Menus are all in English but road signs are for the most part Maltese. Below is a list of a few words that may be helpful.

hotel	lukanda	toilet/bathroom	kamra tal banju
room	kamra	shower	docċa
...single/double	singlu/doppja	balcony	gallarija
...one/two nights	lejl/żewġ iljieli	reception	'reception'
... per person/per room	kull persuna/kull kamra	key	ċavetta
reservation	riserva	room service	servizz fil-kamra
rate	rata	chambermaid	kamriera
breakfast	l-ewwel ikla tal-jum		

bank	bank	American dollar	dollaru Amerikan
exchange office	ufficju tal-kambju	banknote	karta tal-flus
post office	posta	coin	munita
cashier	kaxxier	credit card	karta ta' kredtu
foreign exchange	ufficju tal-kambju	cheque book	'cheque book'
foreign currency	flus barranin	exchange rate	rata tal-kambju
pound sterling	lira sterlina	commission charge	senserija

restaurant	restorant	dinner	ikla
café	café	starter	'starter'
table	majda	main course	ikla
menu	menu	dessert	deserta
set menu	menu fiss	drink	xorb
wine list	lista ta' l-inbid	waiter	waiter
lunch	kolazzjonn	the bill	kont

aeroplane	ajruplan	ticket	biljett
airport	ajruport	...return/single	single/bur-ritorn
bus	karozza tal-linja	...first/second class	l-ewwl/tlieni klassi
...station	stazzjon tal karozza tal-linja	ticket office	ufficju tal biljetti
		timetable	orarju
station	stazzjon tal	seat	seat/post
ferry	ferrovija	non-smoking	tpejjipx
...terminal	vapur terminal	reserved	riservat

yes	iva	help!	ajjut!
no	le	today	illum
please	jekk jogħġbok	tomorrow	għada
thank you	grazzi	yesterday	il-bieraħ
hello	merħba	how much?	kemm?
goodbye	saħħa	expensive	għoli
goodnight	bonswa	open	miftuħ
sorry	jiddispjaċini	closed	magħluq

REMEMBER

- Contact the airport, airline or travel representative on the day prior to leaving to ensure flights are unchanged.

- Arrive 90 minutes before your schedulded flight departure time (particularly during summer) or you may lose your flight.

- Departing visitors must complete an Embarkation Card (available at check-in area) to present at passport control.

Index

TwinPack
Malta & Gozo

Written and updated by Pat Levy and Sean Sheehan
Edited, designed and produced by AA Publishing

Published by AA Publishing, a trading name of Automobile Association Developments Limited, whose registered office is Southwood East, Apollo Rise, Farnborough, Hampshire, GU14 0JW. Registered number 1878835.

The contents of this book are believed correct at the time of printing. Nevertheless, the publishers cannot be held responsible for any errors or omissions or for changes in the details given in this guide or for the consequences of any reliance on the information it provides. Assessments of attractions, hotels, restaurants and other sights are based upon the author's personal experience and, therefore, necessarily contain elements of subjective opinion which may not reflect the publishers' opinion or dictate a reader's own experiences on another occasion.

We have tried to ensure accuracy in this guide, but things do change and we would be grateful if readers would advise us of any inaccuracies they may encounter.

Material in this book may have appeared in other AA publications.

A CIP catalogue record for this book is available from the British Library.

ISBN-10: 0 7495 4342 6
ISBN-13: 978 0 7495 4342 6

Colour separation by Keenes, Andover
Printed and bound by Times Publishing Limited, Malaysia

ACKNOWLEDGEMENTS
The Automobile Association wishes to thank the following libraries and photographers for their assistance in the preparation of this book.

THE ART ARCHIVE 34t, 34b, 40t; PAUL MURPHY 56; VISIT MALTA 6, 7c, 8, 15b, 24t, 27t, 27b, 33t, 40br, 41b, 44t, 45b, 48t, 60t, 60b; MRI BANKERS' GUIDE TO FOREIGN CURRENCY 87.

The remaining pictures used in this publication are held in the Automobile Association's own photo library (AA PHOTO LIBRARY) and were taken by the following photographers:
PHILIP ENTICKNAP F/Cover (a) luzzu, (e) fish platter, (f) Maltese dancer, bottom tomatoes, Marsaxlokk market, Back cover ct (shops), cb (food), 5b, 9, 12t, 12c, 13b, 21t, 23t, 25b, 29t, 29b, 30b, 31, 32b, 33b, 35b, 37t, 39t, 42t, 43t, 44b, 47b, 49b, 52t, 57, 58t, 61t, 84, 90cr; ALEX KOUPRIANOFF F/Cover (b) flag, (c) street lamp, (g) Marfa Ridge Red Tower, Back cover b (neon sign), 7t, 12ct, 15c, 16, 17cb, 17b, 18c, 18b, 19, 20, 24c, 25t, 26t, 26b, 30t, 32t, 35t, 36b, 38t, 38bl, 38br, 39b, 42b. 43b, 45t, 46t, 46b, 47t, 48c, 48b, 50, 51t, 51b, 52b, 53, 54, 55t, 55b, 58b, 59, 85t, 90t; DAVID VINCENT 21b; WYN VOYSEY F/Cover (d) Festival banner, Back cover t (cathedral), 1, 7b, 12b, 13t, 14, 23b, 28t, 28b, 36t, 37b, 40bl, 41t, 49t, 61b, 85b, 90cl.

A02011
Fold out map © Freytag–Berndt u. Artaria KG, 1231 Vienna–Austria, all rights reserved

TITLES IN THE TWINPACK SERIES
• Algarve • Corfu • Costa Blanca • Costa del Sol • Cyprus • Gran Canaria •
• Lanzarote & Fuerteventura • Madeira • Mallorca • Malta & Gozo • Menorca • Tenerife •

Dear **TwinPack** Traveller

Your comments, opinions and recommendations are very important to us. So please help us to improve our travel guides by taking a few minutes to complete this simple questionnaire.

You do not need a stamp (unless posted outside the UK). If you do not want to cut this page from your guide, then photocopy it or write your answers on a plain sheet of paper.

Send to: **The Editor, AA TwinPack Travel Guides, FREEPOST SCE 4598, Basingstoke RG21 4GY.**

Your recommendations…

We always encourage readers' recommendations for restaurants, nightlife or shopping – if your recommendation is used in the next edition of the guide, we will send you a **FREE AA TwinPack Guide** of your choice. Please state below the establishment name, location and your reasons for recommending it.

_____

_____

_____

_____

Please send me **AA TwinPack**

Algarve ❑ Corfu ❑ Costa Blanca ❑ Costa del Sol ❑ Cyprus ❑ Gran Canaria ❑ Lanzarote & Fuerteventura ❑ Madeira ❑ Mallorca ❑ Malta & Gozo ❑ Menorca ❑ Tenerife ❑

(*please tick as appropriate*)

About this guide…

Which title did you buy?
AA *TwinPack* _____

Where did you buy it? _____

When? m m / y y

Why did you choose an AA *TwinPack* Guide? _____

_____

_____

_____

Did this guide meet your expectations?

Exceeded ❑   Met all ❑   Met most ❑   Fell below ❑

Please give your reasons _____

_____

_____

continued on next page…

Were there any aspects of this guide that you particularly liked? _____

_____

_____

Is there anything we could have done better? _____

_____

_____

About you…

Name (*Mr/Mrs/Ms*) _____

    Address _____

_____

_____ Postcode _____

    Daytime tel no _____

Please only give us your mobile phone number if you wish to hear from us about other products and services from the AA and partners by text or mms.

Which age group are you in?

    Under 25 ☐   25–34 ☐   35–44 ☐   45–54 ☐   55–64 ☐   65+ ☐

How many trips do you make a year?

    Less than one ☐   One ☐   Two ☐   Three or more ☐

Are you an AA member? Yes ☐   No ☐

About your trip…

When did you book? m m / y y   When did you travel? m m / y y

How long did you stay? _____

Was it for business or leisure? _____

Did you buy any other travel guides for your trip?

    If yes, which ones? _____

Thank you for taking the time to complete this questionnaire. Please send it to us as soon as possible, and remember, you do not need a stamp (*unless posted outside the UK*).

Happy Holidays!